ARCANA

LAVINIA PINELLO · VALERIA MENOZZI

TAROT
A Card a Day

A PRACTICAL AND INTUITIVE GUIDE

LO SCARABEO

Lavinia Pinello
Valeria Menozzi

TAROT · A CARD A DAY
A practical and intuitive guide

Graphics and layout: Chiara Demagistris
Editing: Elena Delmastro, Riccardo Minetti
Additional texts (Simplicity and Reflections): Riccardo Minetti
Translation: Emily Guidoni
Proofreading: Lunaea Weatherstone

Images: Tarot Original 1909,
by Arthur Edward Waite and Pamela Colman Smith

© 2023 - Lo Scarabeo
Printed by Grafiche Stella

Facebook and Instagram: loscarabeotarot

TABLE OF CONTENTS

SIMPLICITY

This book does not intend to make grandiose revelations nor unveil the meaning of life. Its purpose is rather to gently guide the reader through the discovery of Tarot and of one's inner self.

It is somewhat more humble—playfully humble. A sort of methodology, a useful experiment.

It invites the reader to consider Tarot as something magical. Not magical in an esoteric sense, with all sorts of supernatural mysteries. Magical because the Arcana is a tool that can help all of us (men and women of this urban, technological, industrial, and materialistic civilization) to connect with those intangible parts of existence that we call soul, spirit, or even simply "the psyche"—leading us to a place of spontaneity and intuition, as opposed to a state of determinism and proportionality.

Perhaps the secret of Tarot is just that: its ability to guide us to a mental and spiritual space where we can discover our inner selves. This book, therefore, does not intend to teach a method for reading Tarot cards, nor provide a list of meanings to study. On the contrary, it invites the reader to *experience* Tarot, to include it in their daily life in a natural and harmonious way. If the reader embraces the benefits of this journey, the rest will take care of itself. This is living life, not studying it, like a bird is oblivious to the mechanics of flight, but still knows how to fly.

This process is based on one of the simplest and yet most profound Tarot methodologies: the Card of the Day method. This method requires the reader to devote five minutes a day (preferably in the morning, but evenings are good too) solely to Tarot—no distractions. Moreover, the reader does not need to have any knowledge of Tarot, but simply needs to trust his or her own natural intuition.

As usual when embarking on a journey like this, the very first step is often the hardest to take. After all, the gap between nothing and something is enormous.

Psychologically, making a commitment to working with Tarot cards, perhaps without any guidance other than a book, can be a big hurdle.

We naturally fear the unknown, uncharted waters. Or sometimes it may be the fear of judgment, even our own judgment.

Like all first steps, however, hesitation is simply an illusion created in our own minds. The reader should not see the Card of the Day as a chore, but view it with a more lighthearted, playful spirit, while at the same time seeing it as a challenge. It must be approached without fears or expectations, enjoying and embracing the outcomes with an open mind.

Many of us are accustomed to a form of unconscious thinking that makes us assume that everything profound must also be complicated, or that everything serious and valuable must be boring. In our experience, the opposite is true: simplicity and depth are intimately connected.

So we invite our reader simply to try it out. Profundity will rise to the surface like spring water—not bursting forth in a violent stream, but bubbling out gently and naturally.

THE CARD OF THE DAY METHOD

Take a moment to create a sacred space, where you can be calm and quiet. Take out your Tarot cards, shuffle the deck, and draw a card, then reflect on what you need to be mindful of during the day ahead.

The card will be one of the 78 Arcana. Open the book, read the meaning, or simply look at the image on the card, focusing on what seems important. After a minute or two, at most, put the deck back and continue with your day.

Among the many events of any given day, at some point you will come across an event that evokes the thoughts and the energy of the card you picked that morning. Unlike all the other events of that same day, that one will catch your attention and will be absorbed into your consciousness both superficially and on a deeper level.

In the evening, if you like, re-inspect the morning Tarot card and reflect on the day's event, asking yourself, "What can I learn from this event?" or "What have I gained from this experience?"

The difference between choosing your Card of the Day in the morning or in the evening is minor but still significant. The card selected in the morning draws the reader's attention to a moment during that day. By arousing our perception, the Tarot card triggers our awareness, stimulating it.

On the other hand, if for any reason you cannot find the time or space to select a card in the morning, you can do it at the end of the day. When choosing a card in the evening, you should recall that day's events, and make sure you focus and reflect on them.

THE MECHANICS OF THE METHOD

You may be curious to find out more about the mechanics of the Card of the Day method. Tarot decks, in theory, were created to be a map of human experience. The Major Arcana represent the great stages and themes of life, while the Minor Arcana depict everyday experiences. To find out more, before reading other books or getting bogged down in complex online searches, we advise you to start with "Reflections" at the back of this book, which will probably answer many of the questions you might have.

The Card of the Day method is not based on hard and fast rules or strange deterministic calculations, but instead it is based on *listening*. And this listening brings us back to the concepts of *presence* and *focus*, the foundations of our spiritual nature. It may seem presumptuous to make such a statement, but we exist when we are in a position to perceive the magic of the world.

We all know what our daily lives are like: agitated, neurotic, eventful, sometimes nerve-racking ... this is what our lives are like if we fail to seriously make any changes. Amid all of this, you may find someone asking you in the evening, "Well, how did it go today?" You answer, "Fine," meaning that everything during the day went according to the norm. This "everything," in reality, means "nothing really noteworthy."

Days when nothing significant happens feel like the curse of our existence. But daily life is not truly like that. It is our illusory perception that makes it difficult to notice the wonderful, vivid, meaningful things happening around us all the time.

A blooming flower, a smile, the taste of something, a ray of sunshine, a joke we laughed at, a photograph or drawing, somebody nice we bumped into in the street, a cat purring happily, a song on the radio—everything, viewed from the soul, can be extraordinary. That is the magic of our existence.

By drawing a card from the deck and focusing on it while in that sacred space mentioned above, you are more inclined to open to each event. These can be good or bad, intrusive or transient, obvious or ambiguous. If you focus on these events and they are brought into your consciousness, they truly become an experience; something changes in your life. It becomes part of you. And it is only this way, experience after experience, that we are able to thrive as human beings. However, if they go unnoticed, all we have are simply things that just happened.

It is worthwhile reflecting on the fact that these experiences may also be quite minor and not that easy to identify. For example, imagine you draw the Tower card. This card often has negative connotations, meanings related to destruction and the implosion of the certainties in our lives. It does not, however, mean that you will necessarily witness a building collapsing or some other personal tragedy. It may be something much more subtle. Perhaps, casually walking along the street, you might happen to notice heartbreak on the faces of a teenage couple walking away from each other in opposite directions after an argument. Maybe you look up and see a crack in a ledge. Or you might notice a button come loose on something you have just worn.

But how can these things be considered *experiences*?

This will depend on the reader and the awareness with which they experience them. For instance, the arguing couple might lead you to reflect on your own relationships, to think about the last time you said "I love you" to your partner, or about an argument you had, or words left unspoken. The crack in the ledge could represent the passing of time, which affects everyone, or represent a burden that you sometimes struggle to bear. The button could symbolize the fragility of things and remind you how things change even when you try to keep everything the same.

It could mean all of this, or something different, or even none of this at all.

With the Card of the Day, we ensure that we take a step forward—as human beings—every day.

Realistically speaking, and without wanting to be controversial, we are on the opposite spectrum of whatever is happening in social media. On social media platforms, people transform substance into appearance. On a spiritual path, appearance becomes substance.

THE TAROT

The title of this book, *Tarot - A Card a Day*, seems to suggest that the Card of the Day method helps us to understand Tarot, and it does! But how?

The reader may already have realized that the meaning of Tarot is not necessarily the meaning found in books or Tarot card instructions. Those are just some of the possible keys, certainly not the only ones.

Through its interpretation, Tarot must be able to communicate with our deepest consciousness and penetrate our personal realm. Simply put, it must be able to connect with our experiences, in a way that we can acknowledge them and therefore apply more meaning to our lives.

By using this method daily, the reader will progressively learn to consistently associate Tarot cards and their energy with real life. With each image on the card, our intuition will slowly master the art of connecting the symbolic (the Tarot card) with the experienced events (daily events and the experiences they create). This is a cumulative process. We should not study but internalize. No need to make a conscious effort to memorize—rather, try to acquire in-depth knowledge that is truly part of your consciousness.

Day by day, not only will the reader acquire greater knowledge of Tarot, but more importantly, their understanding of it will expand—to the point of being able to break free from the limits of a book, no matter how good it is—and thus move beyond it.

The key is to combine simplicity with consistency.

HOW TO USE THIS BOOK

As the focus of this book is entirely on the Card of the Day, the information and suggestions provided are designed to allow the reader to experience this method not only in its most basic form but also more thoroughly and in more detail. First, we propose a core meaning for each Arcanum.

For instance, take two keywords associated with the Fool card; one is Innocence, the other is Madness, and they are often seen as opposite ends of a spectrum. The reason being is that each Arcanum embraces these concepts as a whole, and they cannot be expressed in one single word. It might seem that both keywords circumscribed an intuitive space around themselves: "The Fool can symbolize either Innocence or Madness, but also everything in between."

Let's look at this example further. We invite the reader to consider the fact that the irresponsible behavior indicated above would be greatly different in children than in adults. This leads us to further reflect upon the fact that adults can sometimes benefit from reconnecting with their inner child. The Fool Arcanum helps shine a light on these thoughts.

As well as essential keywords, there is also a more extensive and descriptive explanation that can help the reader understand the Arcanum.

For the Fool, for example, it reads: "The Fool indicates infinite potential yet to be unleashed. It is a card of profound freedom, which, if used excessively, leads to losing one's reference points."

For each Arcanum, three other keywords follow, which we will call *energies*.

Arguably, this is an obvious metaphor—each Arcanum vibrates with different frequencies, with each frequency corresponding to its own specific aspect, not unlike the way that there are different aspects to people, depending on the psychological sphere in which they move. To give an example, Lavinia, one of this book's coauthors, can be, depending on the moment, Woman, Mother, Writer, or Owner (the latter refers to her cats, just to be clear!). But she is still and always Lavinia, and these "energies" of hers coexist in her while at the same time being different from each other.

When the reader draws a card and synergizes with the Arcanum, they can facilitate that process by deciding which aspect to push most to the fore.

The consequences here are twofold, the first being that choosing one of the different aspects of the Arcanum will lead us to a greater variety of experiences which is extremely useful for a better and more in-depth understanding of an Arcanum. The second—which is even more important—is that the very fact of consciously and being fully aware of making a choice means performing something *magical*. This voluntary choice translates in real terms into prepping the reader to welcome a particular energy or experience into their life, not passively as an observer, but rather as an actor.

Whatever the reader notices during the day—that is, the experience engraved in their mind that evening—will be something they have, to some degree, created themselves. After all, living life does not mean we are puppets of fate, and being humble does not mean being passive.

For each of these energies, the book offers five different insights or keys to their interpretation. These are, in all cases, five seeds—not meant to be read and accepted passively, but to germinate in the reader's consciousness through the Card of the Day method.

· **Today, the day ahead.** A broader view of life, as distinct from individual topics, which sometimes encourages us to see the whole day in its entirety, instead of fragmenting it into distinct moments.

· **Today, in love.** The eternal dance of the human soul. Love is a necessity of the spirit in all its forms, including romantic love with which it is often confused.

· **Today, at work.** Here lie the energies associated with duties, responsibilities, and obligations, but also the potential to express one's creativity and pursue success.

· **Self-reflection.** An invitation to introspect and observe the events of the soul and experience one's inner realm. Often the more spiritual and psychological aspects of a card are found here.

· **A symbol.** A visual reflection, based on a symbol often found on the Arcanum—but be aware, this depends greatly on the deck being used. Many are unconventional and do not use traditional symbols to communicate with the reader.

Some of these seeds, particularly those referring to "today," harken back in tone to the divinatory messages of yesteryear—so-called fortune-telling. The others can be considered *wiser* or—as we say today—*inspirational*, again based on the principle of offering the reader more choice and different opportunities.

Again (and especially in this case, in fact) the reader is invited to choose and freely change, depending on their priorities, needs, concerns, and inspiration. In many ways, the significance of these aspects is entirely intuitive. The concept of "today" is meant to remind the reader of the transience of the present. To quote the Dalai Lama, "There are only two days in the year when nothing can be done. One is yesterday. The other is tomorrow." The present is meant to be lived. In its pain, in its joys, the present is not made to let it pass us by, because only in the present does saying "I am" make sense.

Lightness, the First and Final Thought

Before we leave the reader with the cards, we would like to devote these last few paragraphs to "lightness," not surprisingly one of the energies associated with the Fool, the first card.

Often, when it comes to personal growth and spirituality, it is easy for our ego to lead us to assume a hallowed attitude to what we do. Instead of really growing, we thus find ourselves part of a cult, whose idol tends to be our own belief system and our convictions.

We do not seek to be life coaches, just authors of a Tarot book. However, we feel it is important to convey a message that reminds us that levity—not superficiality—is the key to a long journey. Not instinct, but naturalness and spontaneity.

We invite you to play with Tarot cards, with the Card of the Day, with everything! We invite you to have fun, without getting swamped in the details. Simply create positive experiences and draw them into the core of your being so that they bear fruit.

Innocence · Foolishness

The Fool indicates infinite potential yet to be unleashed.
It is a card of profound freedom, which, if used excessively,
leads to losing one's reference points.

Choose what kind of energy you want to draw from the Fool today:

Lightness, Creativity, Originality

LIGHTNESS

· *Today, the day ahead*—Today is a perfect day to be lighthearted and carefree. Solutions do not come from hard work and discipline, but rather from taking a step back and finding inner harmony and peace.

· *Today, in love*—In love, you should not give too much importance to your partner's words. Problems will pass as fast as a summer rain shower.

· *Today, at work*—In work, small things should not distract you from the bigger picture. Unfortunately, focusing will be a problem. Best to create a space to fantasize and explore new ideas.

· *Self-reflection*—Self-reflection is important. However, a peaceful walk in the fresh air to clear your mind can spark new insights.

· *A symbol*—The symbol you can reflect on is the feather. It shows how much better the mind can live when the constant weight and burden of responsibility are lifted.

CREATIVITY

· *Today, the day ahead*—Why don't you explore the unknown? Today is a good day to try something new, as impractical as it may be. Ideas that arise from instinct may not bring immediate results, but they set in motion processes that will prove successful in the future.

· *Today, in love*—The Fool suggests making spontaneous gestures, speaking your mind with honesty and truth, not just to fill awkward silences.

· *Today, at work*—An opportunity may arise to do something differently than usual. It doesn't cost anything to try, and you needn't be afraid to take a leap of faith.

· *Self-reflection*—Find some time today to do nothing at all. If all your time is filled with familiar, expected situations, nothing new can develop.

· *A symbol*—The symbol you can reflect on is the flower. It represents the ability to see and appreciate the beautiful things happening in and around you.

ORIGINALITY

· *Today, the day ahead*—Today you may find yourself feeling a bit of a maverick. Being unconforming to others' expectations is something to cherish and treasure, regardless of anyone's opinions.

· *Today, in love*—If you can, bring some novelty to your relationship: a place you've never been, words you've never said, a different way of listening. Amaze yourself and you will amaze the person you love.

· *Today, at work*—At work it will be difficult to make clear and precise choices. Perhaps because the timing is not right, perhaps because there is little information, but mostly because you may still be unclear about which direction to head in.

· *Self-reflection*—Make some room for those parts of yourself that you usually keep hidden. Although they might come as a surprise to some, and they might be perceived to be unlike your usual self, you will certainly feel at ease with exposing those mannerisms that differ from the norm.

· *A symbol*—The symbol you can reflect on is the sun. In those difficult moments, when the sky is filled with clouds, the sun still shines above them.

THE MAGICIAN.

Creative Force · Illusion

The Magician represents active action, impulse and taking initiative,
intelligence, strength and skill, something to set in motion and act upon.
It means carrying out and taking responsibility for your duties.

Choose what kind of energy you want to draw from the Magician today:
Initiative, Creativity, Willpower

INITIATIVE

· *Today, the day ahead*—Today is a great day to kick-start your projects. Be your own boss, make everything you do your own choice, and you have the opportunity to do things thoroughly.

· *Today, in love*—The beginning of a friendship or a romantic relationship, an important encounter, or love at first sight will lead to a sincere and constructive love story. Be resourceful.

· *Today, at work*—Take action! Become aware of your influence in the workplace and use it purposefully to achieve the success you are aiming for.

· *Self-reflection*—Look within. In yourself you can find the tools to shape your own destiny responsibly, consciously, and purposefully to accomplish every task in life.

· *A symbol*—The Magician is firmly holding a wand with his arm raised to the sky. This represents how thought precedes any action.

CREATIVITY

· *Today, the day ahead*—Remember that you are powerful. When you make changes within yourself, the world around you also changes.

· *Today, in love*—Don't just sit around waiting for love to appear—today you can actively create the opportunity to make that encounter happen. For those already in a relationship, focus on ways you can spark things up.

· *Today, at work*—In the career sphere, this symbolizes an idea being conceived—the start of a project or the solution to a problem. What skills do you have? What qualities are you not maximizing to reach your full potential? Being creative can really boost your chances for success.

· *Self-reflection*—Nothing comes from nothing. For dreams to come true you must focus on the ones that mean the most to you. Feed your intellect and use your willpower to organize your life and environment, as well as your mind. The creative power of the mind can be astonishing.

· *A symbol*—On the table in front of him are his tools, the four suits of cards representing the four elements. These symbolize the importance of using both your head and your heart when dealing with day-to-day affairs, as well as doing what you need to do to nourish your body and soul. This is what creative thinking needs to manifest your thoughts into being.

WILLPOWER

· *Today, the day ahead*—Your willpower will help you find the determination you need to commit to achieving your goals.

· *Today, in love*—Although a perfect date can leave a flawless first impression, you should really take the time to get to know your partner or partner-to-be properly. This will help avoid disappointment.

· *Today, at work*—You may lack the determination to turn your talents into money, but don't waste them. There are probably many opportunities to advance. All it might take is a little boost in confidence to really put yourself out there.

· *Self-reflection*—You feel it's time to tap into your full potential to make a big change. Don't hold back—that could mean missing out on the opportunity to become the best version of yourself. On the other hand, don't let it dominate you by becoming an obsession, as that might lead to bad, ill-considered decisions.

· *A symbol*—The symbol you can reflect on today is the infinity symbol. It represents how you can harness the energy of the divine realm and bring it to the earthly plane to manifest your heart's desires.

Wisdom · Interiority

The High Priestess represents inner wisdom.
She invites you to listen to your intuition, accept fate with confidence,
and face the array of life's events with patience and resilience.

Choose what kind of energy you want to draw from the High Priestess today:

Knowledge, Sensitivity, Mystery

KNOWLEDGE

· *Today, the day ahead*—Embedded in every stage of life is a lesson to be learned and cherished. Accepting fate doesn't necessarily mean resignation, but rather having wisdom.

· *Today, in love*—"Silence speaks a thousand words." Truly emotionally connected hearts know how to understand each other even in silence. They know each other's needs and limits and understand when to give advice and when a listening ear is simply the only thing that's needed.

· *Today, at work*—Learning something new might be required. In fact, keeping up to date with current changes and trends demands study, patience, and dedication.

· *Self-reflection*—Need a message from your inner wisdom? Open a book to a random page, read the first full sentence on that page, and use it as inspiration—reflect on its meaning. It might hold an important message.

· *A symbol*—The symbol you can reflect on today is the book. It represents your destiny: life is like a blank canvas, and it is up to you how you want to fill it.

SENSITIVITY

· *Today, the day ahead*—You may feel particularly vulnerable today and because of this you could come across as a little withdrawn. Speaking out and expressing your emotions is always healthier than bottling things up.

· *Today, in love*—In love, try not to be too hasty. Sometimes grace and patience are needed for a strong connection to develop. When it does, the time will have been worthwhile.

· *Today, at work*—Full presence will likely be required in the workplace today. Showing interest, dedication, and attention can help you achieve new goals and objectives.

· *Self-reflection*—While it's okay to be willing to see to others' needs, it should not come at the expense of your own well-being. Sometimes you need to carve out your own space and prioritize your own needs.

· *A symbol*—The symbol to reflect on today is the pomegranate. Just as this fruit hides its precious and delicate seeds within its hard husk, also tend to hide their vulnerabilities behind a strong appearance. Learn to look below the surface.

MYSTERY

· *Today, the day ahead*—This could be the right day to test your limits, explore new things, engage in unusual or intriguing activities.

· *Today, in love*—Don't reveal too much all at once; let your partner discover you slowly. A healthy dose of mystery generates interest and attraction, while things that are obvious and taken for granted risk losing their charm.

· *Today, at work*—If you have a new project in mind, keep it to yourself for now. Better evaluate and define every detail before talking about it with others. You will boost your authenticity and inventiveness.

· *Self-reflection*—Whatever is hidden in your heart—whether it is an unmentionable secret, a dream, a hope, a vulnerability, a memory—don't feel obliged to reveal it. Intimacy is sacred, and no one can force you to reveal yourself.

· *A symbol*—The symbol to meditate on today is the cross. It isn't only your body that needs nourishment but also your soul. It feeds on the experiences you have in life, day after day.

Abundance · Frivolity

The Empress indicates that you are treading on fertile ground,
filled with abundance and novelty. It represents creative processes,
vital growth, and the birth of the new.

Choose what kind of energy you want to draw from the Empress today:

Fertility, Birth, Caring

FERTILITY

· *Today, the day ahead*—Today you can rejoice in the birth of something new and believe in a new process of growth.

· *Today, in love*—You could give the growth of your relationship a boost, nurturing it with warm sensuality. For those hoping for it, a baby might be on its way.

· *Today, at work*—Ahead of you is a prosperous phase that will offer an abundance of possibilities. Prepare the way for dreams to be pursued: you will see them soon come true.

· *Self-reflection*—Currently, you are in a phase of creativity where you nurture new ideas and carry them within you. Take the time to uncover and reveal the ideas that still reside deep within you, and make a commitment to bring them to fruition, believing in your abilities.

· *A symbol*—The symbol to reflect upon today is the pomegranate, an icon of nourishment and fruitfulness. By showing kindness as well as self-care, you will bestow happiness and joy in abundance not only on yourself but also on those around you.

BIRTH

· *Today, the day ahead*—Amidst life's cyclical nature, the ceaseless emergence of new beginnings speaks of your ever-changing existence, calling you to endure the challenges of rebirth.

· *Today, in love*—An important meeting is a possibility, a new relationship that blossoms under the banner of gentleness and loyalty.

· *Today, at work*—You will seek innovation, growth, and resourcefulness in other professional spheres. It would be wise to prepare yourself for changes in your work environment and anticipate the possibility of new challenges that may divert you from your normal routine. Although the initial stages of this transformation may seem arduous, with smart and methodical work, success will come swiftly.

· *Self-reflection*—On the plane of consciousness, you are afforded new perspectives and insights that may or may not seem pleasant but are nonetheless enriching. Such experiences illuminate the perpetual ebb and flow of life, demonstrating that nothing is permanent, and that for every ending, there is a new beginning.

· *A symbol*—The symbol you can reflect on is nature. Blooming nature surrounds the Empress symbolizing the cyclical nature of existence, where all things are born, flourish, and ultimately perish, paving the way for new beginnings. Embracing this inevitable truth is essential.

CARING

· *Today, the day ahead*—Your disposition leans toward motherly, nurturing, and compassionate, which creates a sense of security and support for those around you. However, it is crucial to avoid over-extending yourself by neglecting your own needs or overwhelming your loved ones, albeit with good intentions.

· *Today, in love*—Spending quality time with your partner is important to fuel the passionate momentum that is part of your relationship. Take care of each other in small daily gestures, even if it's just carving out time to take a simple walk holding hands; you will benefit.

· *Today, at work*—You could try to make your workplace more harmonious and welcoming—whether that means supporting colleagues or applying a new coat of paint in your office or at home. Creating a positive and warm environment can make your workplace more stimulating.

· *Self-reflection*—Others see that side of you that would like to express itself creatively. If such a side of your nature is unknown to you, nurture and cherish it. You'll be amazed at the advantages this can bring you.

· *A symbol*—Reflect on the symbol for Venus today and let it inspire you to passionately love yourself and the world around you. Nurture this love, relish life, and be willing to freely go with the flow of life.

Governing · Authority

The Emperor represents the ability to govern, discipline, and command. It symbolizes an extremely stable, secure, and grounded character, albeit a little too materialistic and dominant at times.

Choose what kind of energy you want to draw from the Emperor today:

Power, Order, Stability

POWER

· *Today, the day ahead*—You'll likely need a lot of commitment and determination throughout the day. You should set goals and establish boundaries, both for yourself and for those around you.

· *Today, in love*—Loving someone does not mean controlling or dominating them, but rather giving them the freedom to express themselves and realize their potential. Power struggles can damage relationships, while mutual respect and appreciation can help to strengthen them.

· *Today, at work*—It's important to maintain a sense of authority in the workplace today. However, this doesn't mean being overly authoritarian. A good leader knows how to consider the opinions of their colleagues and subordinates and value them.

· *Self-reflection*—To reach your goals, it's important to set yourself limits and rules. But if you're too harsh about this, you might miss out on the joys of life's simple pleasures. They key is to not be overly strict with yourself.

· *A symbol*—Reflecting on the symbol of the scepter today can remind you of the qualities needed to be in control of your life: strength, self-esteem, integrity, wisdom, and determination.

ORDER

· *Today, the day ahead*—Today is the time to take a step back and assess the situation, prioritize tasks, set deadlines, and make your projects tangible. Only then can you complete what you started and reap the rewards of your hard work.

· *Today, in love*—It's important for both members of a couple to give and receive from each other. When this balance is disrupted, it can be difficult to maintain trust and respect. Take some time to think about the balance in your relationship. What can you do to restore it?

· *Today, at work*—If it looks like it's going to be a stressful day, try to get organized before you start working hard. Doing this will help you gain clarity, save time, and avoid any unnecessary details or complications.

· *Self-reflection*—What's keeping you from feeling truly fulfilled? Is it the opinions of others, your lack of self-confidence, or the irrational belief that you won't be able to achieve your goals? Don't be so hard on yourself—have faith in yourself and your abilities!

· *A symbol*—Today's symbol is the ram's head, representing the tenacity and strength to break through boundaries and overcome obstacles. Just like the ram, you too can achieve your goals if you put your mind to it. Believe in yourself and remember: anything is possible if you want it enough.

STABILITY

· *Today, the day ahead*—Today you will be able to solve some practical problems if you work hard and are serious about finishing everything you have started. Don't waste any time.

· *Today, in love*—While a stable and mature relationship doesn't need constant reassurance, this doesn't mean you can forget about showing your partner love and affection. Why not surprise them with a romantic gesture or a heartfelt compliment every now and then?

· *Today, at work*—We all strive for financial stability, but dedicating your life solely to work without taking time for leisure and relaxation won't make you any happier. Don't get too caught up in materialism.

· *Self-reflection*—Today, challenge yourself to do something out of the ordinary and not too strenuous—it can be incredibly invigorating and rewarding.

· *A symbol*—Reflect on the throne symbol today. To find contentment and peace, you need a strong and secure foundation. If you haven't been given that, you can still build it now.

THE HIEROPHANT

Knowledge · Sincerity · Rebellion

The Hierophant symbolizes the quest to uncover the profound purpose of life, acting as a mentor to help you understand the things that truly matter. He stands for strong moral values and encourages you to take the path of trust and faith, which will ultimately lead to a rewarding experience.

Choose what kind of energy you want to draw from the Hierophant today:

Tradition, Wisdom, Determination

TRADITION

· *Today, the day ahead*—Keep common sense in mind and have the confidence to do the right thing in any situation.

· *Today, in love*—Your moral values and personal virtues should guide your actions within your relationship. If you feel it's the right thing to do, don't hesitate to take the next step and make your union official with marriage.

· *Today, at work*—Your creativity, success, and freedom in the workplace may be hindered by bureaucracy, processes, or rules. You may feel like you're being held back and have no room to maneuver. Consider the potential risks of going against the grain, but also ask yourself if you can remain true to your beliefs while staying in your current position.

· *Self-reflection*—At times in life, you may feel the need to take the safe route, to lean on the social structures and traditions that you are familiar with. This doesn't mean conformity, but rather finding comfort in following a process that is well known and perhaps even established by you.

· *A symbol*—Reflect on the symbolism of keys. They represent the power of tradition and conformity that exists in the world, where the spiritual and the physical realms entwine. With wisdom and trust, you can unlock many doors and allow a smooth passage between them.

WISDOM

· *Today, the day ahead*—When you are surrounded by words of wisdom, meaningful advice, and moral teachings—through education, learning, contemplation, and spiritual practice—the earthly and heavenly realms are united.

· *Today, in love*—It's important to understand and be understood in a relationship. Don't act impulsively; instead, talk to the people you trust and speak with the most, as they can give you practical advice on how to move forward.

· *Today, at work*—At work, you can invest in further education by attending a school or vocational training course, or by seeking out a mentor with more experience. This could be a great way to help you progress in your career.

· *Self-reflection*—Reflecting on the purpose of life and considering your faith, principles, and values should be a deeply personal experience which is not open to the opinion of others, without this diminishing its value or importance in any way.

· *A symbol*—Reflecting on the symbol of the two columns today can remind you of the importance of finding a balance between opposing forces. It takes a mature and wise approach to navigate between them, without being restricted by either side. It takes a certain level of detachment and a gentle wisdom to be able to observe the world with a smile.

DETERMINATION

· *Today, the day ahead*—Achieving a healthy balance of mental and physical well-being means being able to approach life's challenges with clarity and strength. This self-assurance and maturity allow you to live in harmony with the world around you and find satisfaction in your life.

· *Today, in love*—Your relationship is characterized by maturity, serenity, and conscious decision-making. You both value your roles as leaders and strive to keep your promises to one another.

· *Today, at work*—You may be tempted to take risks and try out new ways of making money, but if you take a step back and look at the situation with a long-term perspective, you will find the strength to stay on the course you have chosen, staying true to your values.

· *Self-reflection*—Don't be scared; life has many paths, and you'll meet lots of people along the way. You'll have plenty of choices to make, and it's okay if you make mistakes. Listen to your inner voice and ask questions if you're unsure. Take control of your life and keep going.

· *A symbol*—Reflecting on the symbol of the scepter today can help you find the purposeful balance to hold your own existence. With discernment, you can find that balance.

Falling in Love · Crossroads

The Arcanum of the Lovers is all about emotions and the choices
you make. It's a reminder that when it comes to decisions,
it's best to follow your heart.

Choose what kind of energy you want to draw from the Lovers today:
Choice, Love, Union

CHOICE

· *Today, the day ahead*—Stop beating yourself up over inner conflicts and Hamletic doubts! Today you can finally make a decision that will make you feel good and lift your spirits.

· *Today, in love*—When making decisions as a couple, big or small, it's important to consider both of your well-beings. Don't let fear of disappointing your partner stop you from making decisions that are best for you both.

· *Today, at work*—Today, you may have to make some important decisions. If you're feeling uncertain, think about which option will make you feel the best and lighten your load. Don't worry—you will make the right choice!

· *Self-reflection*—Sometimes it's better not to try to please everyone else at the cost of your own well-being. Today, take a moment to think about yourself and what you need.

· *A symbol*—Reflect on the symbol of the apple today. Every decision you make has consequences, so if you follow your heart, the outcome will be more manageable. Don't procrastinate—act now.

LOVE

· *Today, the day ahead*—Today is a great opportunity to reflect on whether you have achieved your goals in life, pursued your passions, and devoted yourself to what you have always been passionate about. It's never too late to rediscover your true self.

· *Today, in love*—Oh yes, the heart is alive today! Whether it's for a new love, an old flame, or just love in general, it doesn't matter: everything will feel more vibrant and alive.

· *Today, at work*—Today is a great day to work in a peaceful and collaborative atmosphere. It's a perfect opportunity to involve others in enjoyable and not overly demanding tasks.

· *Self-reflection*—Today is the perfect day to give your passions some attention. It's important to fulfill your responsibilities, but it's also important to make time for the things that bring you joy. Your mind and body will thank you for it.

· *A symbol*—The symbol you can reflect on is the angel. When love calls, you may try to run away, ignore it, or deny it, but eventually you will have to listen and succumb to its immense power.

· *Today, the day ahead*—Today is the ideal time to embrace new experiences with enthusiasm and an open mind. Don't limit yourself from what life has to offer.

· *Today, in love*—Today could be the perfect opportunity to do something enjoyable and calming with your significant other. It doesn't take much to reignite the spark and strengthen your bond.

· *Today, at work*—Breaking down tasks and organizing them can help you make the most of your time and increase your productivity. Don't try to do everything by yourself; two heads are better than one!

· *Self-reflection*—If you find yourself in a situation where your mind and heart are in conflict, take a step back and give yourself time to gain clarity. Prioritize what makes you feel good, even if it may seem unnecessary at first. Once you have a clearer understanding of the situation, solutions will come to you almost magically.

· *A symbol*—Reflecting on the symbol of nakedness can help you understand the importance of transparency in your relationships. When you take off your masks and reveal your true self, you can create meaningful and genuine connections with others.

Victory · Journey

The Chariot symbolizes the power of self-discovery and the joy of embarking on a new journey. It can signify how conflicting forces must be reconciled to make a significant advancement. It can also serve as a reminder to not overestimate your capabilities.

Choose what kind of energy you want to draw from the Chariot today:

Movement, Self-Discipline, Action

MOVEMENT

· *Today, the day ahead*—Focus all your energy and tackle any problems as if you were delivering a knockout punch. Don't be intimidated; it's not about what you leave behind, but rather where you want to go.

· *Today, in love*—Stagnant relationships are destined to eventually fade. Today could be a great opportunity to spice up your relationship: try planning a fun activity together, like a day out somewhere. It could also be the perfect time to start a long-distance relationship.

· *Today, at work*—Nothing comes from nothing. Now is the time to get started and build up momentum toward your career goals. You know what you want to achieve, so stay focused and you'll be sure to reach it.

· *Self-reflection*—You feel like you're on the cusp of a new, exciting journey filled with new opportunities and experiences. You're eager to break away from any stagnation and have the energy to inject some new life into your life.

· *A symbol*—Reflect on the symbol of the road today. Don't worry about leaving your comfort zone behind; you can always return to it later if necessary.

SELF-DISCIPLINE

· *Today, the day ahead*—You have the best of intentions, the drive to act, and goals to reach, but sometimes you can get sidetracked and end up not achieving what you set out to do. Stay focused and determined and you'll get there!

· *Today, in love*—When it comes to love, you may find yourself struggling between two powerful, yet opposing, desires. It's important to stay in control and stay on your chosen path. Ultimately, you are the only one who can decide what's best for you.

· *Today, at work*—Try to stay focused and avoid distractions, whether they come from company policies or rivalries between colleagues. Persevere with dedication and commitment.

· *Self-reflection*—Your strong-willed personality is a combination of both rational and emotional components. Finding the right balance between these two sides of your personality can be challenging, but with determination and perseverance, you can accomplish anything you set your mind to.

· *A symbol*—Today's symbol is the two sphinxes, symbolizing the need to maintain a balance between rationality and emotions.

ACTION

· *Today, the day ahead*—It is time to act swiftly and decisively. Preparations have been made, plans have been laid out, and there is no more time for hesitation.

· *Today, in love*—Make sure you have a good grasp of what you want in terms of love and romance, then act. Now could be a great time to start creating a life for two, or to take a chance on something new and get back into the dating game.

· *Today, at work*—Deadlines are looming, and important dates are fast approaching. Now is not the time to procrastinate—you must act quickly to seize the opportunity that is right in front of you!

· *Self-reflection*— You can't seem to stay still today. You feel an urge to keep moving, to do something no matter what. While it can be a good way to release energy, take a moment to ask yourself why you're feeling so restless.

· *A symbol*—Reflecting on the symbol of the chariot driver today can help you to act effectively. Once you have chosen a direction and a plan of action, you no longer need to move forward with ardor and eagerness. You can take careful aim at your target, just like shooting an arrow.

Courage · Struggle

Strength symbolizes the harmonious relationship between humans and nature. Use your loving power to tame the wildness of your instinctual passions, keeping them in balance so that they do not become overwhelming. Having a caring relationship with nature reflects inner strength.

Choose what kind of energy you want to draw from Strength today:

Leadership, Passion, Courage

LEADERSHIP

· *Today, the day ahead*—Today, you can rely on your magnetic personality, your inner strength, your ability to motivate and inspire, and your intelligence to take control of situations and influence those around you.

· *Today, in love*—When it comes to love, it's important to remain in control. Use the tools available to you wisely and with caution. Showing empathy and having inner strength are essential qualities that will bring you and your partner closer together.

· *Today, at work*—At work, you have the ability to not only face challenges head-on, but also to take charge of them, without letting them overpower you. Your charisma draws the best people to your team.

· *Self-reflection*—Facts show that having character doesn't mean dominance. Instead, it means being self-confident and not afraid to show your true identity. It is about having emotional and psychological resilience.

· *A symbol*—Reflecting on the symbol of the sky today can remind you that true strength comes from within, rather than being a mere external display. It is an attitude, rather than a power, that comes from deep within you.

PASSION

· *Today, the day ahead*—Don't try to cover up your true self with a facade of false virtue. Instead, embrace your instincts and work to gain control over them. By doing this, you will be able to access both your inner strength and the energy you have been using to repress your true nature. Channel that energy with love and you will be able to guide yourself in the right direction.

· *Today, in love*—This card suggests that you may be in a passionate and fiery love story. The strong emotions associated with this card could indicate a relationship that is full of intensity, whether it be in a positive or negative way. You may experience strong feelings of love but also be prone to anger, jealousy, or other emotional outbursts.

· *Today, at work*—If you can tap into your natural animal instincts, such as rage, energy, and passion, you can make great strides in your career. Rather than letting these instincts take control, try to work with them and use them to your advantage. Channeling them into a productive use can help you reach your goals.

· *Self-reflection*—You should not judge or reject your lower instincts, but rather strive to reconcile your conscious and animal selves in three ways: by overcoming the conflict, by preserving those energies to keep them alive, and by elevating them to a point where they no longer oppose each other but instead combine to form an unstoppable force.

· *A symbol*—Today, reflect on the symbol of the lion. It symbolizes animal instinct, desire, and passion, but also jealousy and anger that can arise uncontrollably in certain life situations. However, if you look closely, it appears to be tamed. This suggests that Strength has been able to control, without destroying, its own animal instincts and has drawn a powerful energy from them.

COURAGE

· *Today, the day ahead*—Today, your courage and resilience will serve you well. Your boldness shows that you should have no trouble expressing your thoughts.

· *Today, in love*—Your loyalty and determination are rewarded! You have nothing to worry about when it comes to the sincerity and commitment of your partner. Your tenacity and strength will help you overcome any difficulties that may arise.

· *Today, at work*—Gather your inner strength and take bold steps. If you're aiming for a promotion, do something to make yourself stand out. If you're looking to switch up your career, don't be afraid to give it a go. And if you've been dreaming of starting your own business, take that first step and get started.

· *Self-reflection*—You have the strength and courage to confront your fears and overcome them without letting them take control of you.

· *A symbol*—Reflecting on the symbol of the maiden today can be a reminder that courage comes from within. A delicate young woman cannot rely on physical strength but instead must draw on her inner calm, self-confidence, and courage to face difficult situations. The maiden's example of opening the jaws of the lion is a testament to this inner strength.

Note: In some decks—particularly in the French versions, such as the Tarot de Marseille—Strength appears with the number XI.

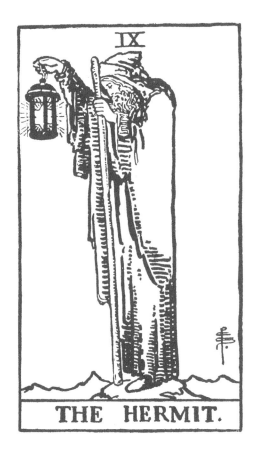

Solitude · Maturity

The Hermit card symbolizes the journey of those who have chosen
a spiritual path, often one that is not straightforward or easy.
It represents a need for contemplation, detachment from material
possessions, and a disconnection from worldly events.

Choose what kind of energy you want to draw from the Hermit today:

Seclusion, Search, Overcoming Crisis

SECLUSION

· *Today, the day ahead*—You have a lot of friends, a packed schedule, and a great social life, but sometimes you still feel like something is missing. Perhaps you feel like you've lost sight of your goals? Taking a day to yourself could be just what you need. Switch off your phone, take some time to yourself, and reconnect with your deepest desires.

· *Today, in love*—If the Hermit card appears in your reading, it may be a sign that you need to take some time for yourself. If you're not in a relationship, don't feel pressured to rush into one; love can wait. If you are in a relationship, let your partner know that you need some time alone. Reassure them that this is just a temporary situation and that you'll be more understanding and compassionate tomorrow.

· *Today, at work*—If you're feeling short on patience today, it might be best to delegate public relations tasks to someone else and focus on tasks that don't require too much interaction with colleagues and clients.

· *Self-reflection*—If you want to embark on a spiritual journey of self-discovery, it is important to practice introspection, reflection, and detachment. These skills are difficult to cultivate when you are surrounded by chaos and crowds. Consider taking a break from society and spending some time in solitude to deepen your understanding of yourself.

· *A symbol*—The symbol you can reflect on today is the cloak. It symbolizes divine protection and the ability to find answers within.

SEARCH

· *Today, the day ahead*—If you can manage to find some time in your hectic schedule today, why not take a break and head out of town to enjoy some time in nature, like a forest? You'll feel energized for a good while afterward.

· *Today, in love*—If you're single, don't worry about searching for love right now; focus on making your dreams a reality and your soul mate will come along in due time. If you're in a relationship, give your partner some breathing room and try to avoid nagging.

· *Today, at work*—Have you ever questioned whether your job truly aligns with your calling, or if you're simply pursuing it for economic reasons? At times, finding contentment in a modest yet peaceful professional life can bring greater joy than a flashy but stressful career.

· *Self-reflection*—Looking for a way to quiet your mind and turn your focus inward? Try sitting in a quiet, dark place and fixating your gaze on a lit candle for a while, while attempting to clear your mind of all thoughts. Then try transcribing the images and thoughts that come to mind during this meditative practice.

· *A symbol*—Today's symbol to contemplate is the lantern. This tool, which illuminates the darkness and casts enchanting images outward, symbolizes your inherent need to discover the true meaning of your existence.

OVERCOMING CRISIS

· *Today, the day ahead*—Remember, dwelling on the past and isolating yourself from the world won't help you emerge from a difficult period. Sometimes all it takes is an honest conversation with a close friend to find a glimmer of hope.

· *Today, in love*—Just as a single rock can't withstand the force of the sea, a minor crisis won't destroy a solid relationship. Some time alone can clear the air and strengthen your bond.

· *Today, at work*—It's time to slow down, take stock, and plan for the future. Have you started saving for retirement? Remember, what you sow today, you'll reap tomorrow.

· *Self-reflection*—At any point in life, it's possible to face an existential crisis. In those seemingly dark moments, focus on what's truly essential for your growth and discard the rest.

· *A symbol*—The symbol to meditate on today is the staff. This simple object, which can serve as a beggar's humble support or a king's potent symbol of power, reminds us that we alone determine how we use the opportunities life presents us.

WHEEL of FORTUNE.

Destiny · Change

The Wheel of Fortune represents the cyclical nature of human destiny, where individuals may experience great heights one moment and plummet toward the depths the next. It's a powerful reminder that everything is impermanent, and those who resist this universal truth often suffer the most.

Choose what kind of energy you want to draw from the Wheel of Fortune today:

Change, Pause, Fortune

CHANGE

· *Today, the day ahead*—Breaking habits can be rejuvenating, so why not treat yourself to something new today, no matter how big or small? It could be as simple as walking instead of driving, taking a different route, or wearing a color you don't typically wear.

· *Today, in love*—Doing something out of the ordinary can reignite the spark in your relationship, so why not break the routine today and surprise your partner? Show them that you don't feel burdened by the passing of time and daily grind.

· *Today, at work*—Don't panic if you find yourself performing a new task today. Trust in your ability to adapt and give yourself time to learn. Proceed with confidence, knowing that you will acquire new skills along the way.

· *Self-reflection*—Take a moment today to observe yourself in the mirror without judgment. Look at yourself as if you were a friend and appreciate the changes that time has brought to your appearance. Remember that these changes have helped shape the person you are today.

· *A symbol*—The symbols to meditate on today are the eagle, angel, bull, and lion. These symbols represent the four seasons, reminding us that just as nature undergoes cyclical changes, so does human existence. Life is a journey of various stages, from youth to maturity and old age.

PAUSE

· *Today, the day ahead*—To assess the situation, take a break today instead of carrying on with your current tasks or initiating a new project. Use this time to make an impartial evaluation of the circumstances and determine the best course of action.

· *Today, in love*—When it comes to matters of the heart, it's time to take a significant step. You must decide whether to end your relationship or move forward and grow together. Procrastination is no longer an option, so act today.

· *Today, at work*—Today has turned out to be an unproductive day at work, leaving you feeling frustrated and eager to accomplish your tasks. However, due to unforeseen circumstances, there's nothing you can do but relax and wait for a better tomorrow.

· *Self-reflection*—There are times when it feels like fate is testing you by placing obstacles in your path. But don't give up just yet; these obstacles are valuable opportunities for growth and maturity. Once you overcome them, you'll have complete control over your life.

· *A symbol*—The symbol of the wheel can provide food for thought. It represents the cyclical nature of time, through which life sometimes flows steadily and sometimes may encounter necessary halts.

FORTUNE

· *Today, the day ahead*—You may experience a small, delightful stroke of luck without even trying. Embrace it with joy, even if it won't drastically alter your life. It'll likely make you feel good for a moment, so give thanks to fortune for it.

· *Today, in love*—If you're in a relationship, today the chemistry between you and your partner will be perfect. And if you're currently single, there may be a bright and hopeful future on the horizon. There are plenty of reasons to be optimistic and cheerful about love today.

· *Today, at work*—While you may possess experience, knowledge, and expertise in your field of work, they may not be enough to guarantee success. It also requires a bit of luck, so you'll need to be daring and take risks today.

· *Self-reflection*—Although pondering the fleeting nature of fate can be a philosophical pastime, it won't help you move forward. It's time to stop dwelling on the past and start looking ahead. Whatever is meant to happen will happen.

· *A symbol*—Two symbols to reflect on are Seth and Anubis. These two figures appear on either side of the wheel, with a snake pointing downward and a cynocephalic character looking upward. They represent the various directions that life can take, sometimes downward and sometimes upward.

Justice · Neutrality

Justice symbolizes the capacity to assess things critically and fairly. Like the Greek goddess Astraea, who wields a sword and scales, she evaluates the various options that destiny presents and consciously discards anything superfluous.

Choose what kind of energy you want to draw from Justice today:

Equity, Accountability, Judgment

EQUITY

· *Today, the day ahead*—The saying "virtue lies in the middle" applies to your day more than ever. Try to avoid going to extremes.

· *Today, in love*—Take a moment to consider the balance in your relationship. Are responsibilities and rights equal? Do both partners contribute to conversations and displays of affection, or is it one-sided? Does either partner feel like they are giving more than they receive? Think about how you can restore balance.

· *Today, at work*—You will receive fair compensation for your efforts, neither more nor less. Be as objective and critical as possible.

· *Self-reflection*—If someone's behavior at work seems unfair to you, don't hesitate to speak your mind, demand fair recognition, and stand up for yourself.

· *A symbol*—Reflect on the symbol of the sword today. It represents the need to remove anything that causes harm to bring balance and order to your life.

ACCOUNTABILITY

· *Today, the day ahead*—It might be a good idea to make decisions that you've been putting off for a while. Use your critical thinking skills and determination to guide you. While it's important to consider your own interests, don't forget the proverb, "You will reap what you sow."

· *Today, in love*—In case of a minor disagreement with your partner, it's best not to make the situation worse by reacting aggressively. Rather, take responsibility and approach the issue calmly to find a resolution. This approach can prevent further escalation of the conflict and help resolve it quickly.

· *Today, at work*—You will need to rely heavily on your abilities. Although it will require dedication and commitment from you, your hard work will not go unnoticed; your efforts will be recognized and eventually rewarded.

· *Self-reflection*—Be sure to carefully consider any potential consequences before speaking or acting. It is neither proper nor mature to shift the responsibility onto others. You are the only one accountable for your actions throughout life.

· *A symbol*—Reflect on the symbol of the scales. It serves as a reminder that we are all accountable for our actions, and that each action has its own set of consequences that we must accept.

· *Today, the day ahead*—Unfortunately, justice doesn't always prevail in the world. Today, you may feel particularly drawn to issues related to human rights, environmental protection, or other significant social problems.

· *Today, in love*—Your partner may appear reserved today, but don't mistake their silence for hostility. Ask them openly and sincerely about their thoughts, and they will likely answer you honestly.

· *Today, at work*—It's important to use your critical thinking skills today. Don't be overly harsh with yourself or your colleagues, as making mistakes is a part of being human.

· *Self-reflection*—It's not always appropriate to give too much importance to others' opinions. No one knows your life and problems better than you do. Similarly, it's unfair to criticize others' choices without first attempting to understand their perspective.

· *A symbol*—Reflect on the symbol of the crown. The crown of Justice resembles the walls of a fortified city and symbolizes the freedom of choice and action that is inherent in human beings.

Note: *In some decks—particularly in French versions such as the Tarot de Marseille—Justice appears with the number VIII.*

THE HANGED MAN.

Reflection · Stalling

This Arcanum is often misinterpreted. The Hanged Man,
shown upside-down, is not in a state of suffering. Instead, the position
is comfortable and voluntary. This card represents a necessary break,
a moment of calmness, reflection, and reevaluation of one's convictions.

Choose what kind of energy you want to draw from the Hanged Man today:
Different Perspective, Rebirth, Stalling

DIFFERENT PERSPECTIVE

· *Today, the day ahead*—Do you sense that everything is moving in the opposite direction of what feels natural today? It can be challenging to determine if you're making things unnecessarily difficult for yourself or if it is the world out of sync. If you want to avoid unnecessary hardship, pause, take some time to observe and reflect. Avoid overburdening yourself, and patiently wait for the situation to resolve itself.

· *Today, in love*—Sulking and playing the victim won't resolve the situation. The simplest and most mature solution is to adjust your attitude and let go of any unrealistic expectations.

· *Today, at work*—Your ideas may not align with the usual practices at work. Spending your time and energy promoting them would be pointless. While you can choose to stick to your guns, it might be more beneficial to consider the perspectives of others.

· *Self-reflection*—This is an ideal day to engage in meditative physical activities like yoga or tai chi. Afterward, you'll not only feel physically refreshed but also see the world from a different perspective.

· *A symbol*—Contemplate the symbol of the upside-down position. This character's posture serves as a reminder that it can be valuable, even necessary, to view things from a different perspective than usual. Only then can you uncover your true character.

REBIRTH

· *Today, the day ahead*—Throughout our lives, we go through various stages where cycles come to an end and new ones begin. It's almost like experiencing many small deaths and rebirths in succession. The symbolism of the Hanged Man implies that if you're prepared, you can begin a new phase of your life from today and be reborn.

· *Today, in love*—When it comes to love, be open to making small sacrifices if needed. Acknowledging your faults and taking responsibility can prevent minor issues from turning into significant problems. Avoid arguing and focus on listening instead.

· *Today, at work*—It appears to be the appropriate time to explore new solutions. Do you feel prepared to break free from conventional patterns but sense a lack of understanding from others? Don't be too hard on yourself, as new opportunities are on the horizon.

· *Self-reflection*—You don't always require grand gestures to alter a situation; sometimes changing your inner dynamics is enough. Adopting a new perspective can help you get back on track.

· *A symbol*—Contemplate the symbol of the rope tied to the Hanged Man's ankle, which represents an umbilical cord. To allow rebirth, it's sometimes necessary to cut the cords that hold you back.

STALLING

· *Today, the day ahead*—If you feel stuck, don't force things; wait for the right moment to return to action with greater determination.

· *Today, in love*—Something might be holding you back from expressing your needs to your partner. Perhaps you're afraid of pushing your limits too far? Remember that a relationship shouldn't feel like a golden cage.

· *Today, at work*—Take advantage of a static situation to address things you've neglected for a long time. Get rid of unnecessary clutter but be cautious not to dispose of something you may need.

· *Self-reflection*—Attempting to change others' opinions won't get you far. Instead, try to view things from their perspective to make yourself understood and overcome your own biases. Be prepared to embrace change, if possible.

· *A symbol*—Today's symbol to reflect upon is the tree. Just like a tree with strong roots can endure the harsh winter and bear fruit in the summer, you too can overcome any season of life by staying grounded in your goals.

Transformation · End and Beginning

This card, often unjustly feared, represents the end of a cycle that is necessary for a new beginning. It reminds you that what may seem to come to an end on the surface is undergoing a deeper transformation.

Choose what kind of energy you want to draw from Death today:

Radical Change, Necessary End, Letting Go

RADICAL CHANGE

· *Today, the day ahead*—While walking down familiar paths may make you feel more confident, don't you think it's time to explore new horizons or change direction? Embracing novelty may pleasantly surprise you.

· *Today, in love*—Naturally, some dynamics within a couple may no longer be effective. If you and your partner desire to continue the relationship, both of you must be open to making changes. If not, it just might be best to call it a day and move forward.

· *Today, at work*—Do you often find yourself complaining about your job? Do you feel that your relationship with coworkers, your duties, or your salary no longer satisfy you? Before you make any drastic decisions, perhaps you can try making substantial changes in your workplace.

· *Self-reflection*—If you want to steer your life in a different direction, begin with yourself. By learning to step out of your comfort zone, you'll discover a limitless world waiting for you, with an array of doors waiting to be opened.

· *A symbol*—The symbol to contemplate today is the breastplate. Life is not always a bed of roses; we frequently face adversity, deal with trauma, and process grief. Nonetheless, remember that every change you go through makes you stronger and more resilient.

NECESSARY END

· *Today, the day ahead*—Do you wish to see yourself differently and receive admiration for your appearance? Think about updating your style. A daring new haircut might be just what you need.

· *Today, in love*—Hanging on to an unfulfilling relationship takes a toll on both partners. When this is the case, agreeing to part ways is the best solution for both. For every door that closes, another one opens.

· *Today, at work*—You might find that some of your decisions appear overly drastic to others. Stand by them and follow through. After all, it would have only been a matter of time before these uncomfortable decisions had to eventually be made.

· *Self-reflection*—Are you feeling scared about the future now that one phase of your life has ended? Don't worry, it's normal to fear the unknown. However, remember that every new beginning comes from the end of something else.

· *A symbol*—The symbol to contemplate today is the white flower on the black flag. This Arcanum's emblem could be interpreted as a white lotus blooming in a dark pond. Just as flowers can grow beautifully in murky water, so can we blossom from the dark depths of our past mistakes.

LETTING GO

· *Today, the day ahead*—Have you noticed that your closet is overflowing? There's no point in keeping clothes that no longer fit or that you've never worn. Consider giving them away and creating space for a new wardrobe.

· *Today, in love*—When it comes to love, let go of the past. Holding on to regrets, resentments, and remorse can damage love and hinder the growth of a relationship. Try to forgive, make changes where you can, or end the commitment if that's what you need.

· *Today, at work*—If you've been working tirelessly and pushing yourself to the limit, take a break today, unplug, and delegate your tasks. You'll return tomorrow feeling refreshed and more productive than ever.

· *Self-reflection*—Hoarding possessions, thoughts, and emotions can impede the natural flow of energy. Let go of any excess baggage and feel the liberating sensation it gives.

· *A symbol*—The symbol to contemplate today is the horse. In many ancient cultures, this animal represented power and transcendence. It symbolizes the ability to face and overcome life's challenges with courage and dignity.

Moderation · Healing

Within this Arcanum, we witness a winged figure—perhaps a goddess or angel—who demonstrates remarkable skill as she gracefully pours a liquid from one vessel to another, without a single drop being wasted. This image symbolizes the importance of harmonizing conflicting energies and reminds us of the value of a gentle, nonintrusive approach to life.

Choose what kind of energy you want to draw from Temperance today:

Diplomacy, Healing, Harmony

DIPLOMACY

· *Today, the day ahead*—It's wise to maintain a calm demeanor today and consider making small compromises if needed. Your composure has the potential to spread to those around you, cultivating a tranquil and harmonious atmosphere in your immediate environment.

· *Today, in love*—By being receptive to communication today, you can foster an atmosphere of serenity and tolerance within your relationship. If there seems to be tension in the air, it may be best to wait for your partner to initiate conversation.

· *Today, at work*—It's not recommended to take extreme stances. If you find yourself assigned to lengthy or repetitive tasks, it's important to maintain a healthy balance and not overexert yourself. Remember to approach the situation with a philosophical outlook.

· *Self-reflection*—Now is not the time to indulge in extravagance, but neither is it the time for extreme renunciation. It's been said that *"in medio stat virtus,"* which translates to "virtue lies in the middle." This reminds us that the best course of action is often a balanced one.

· *A symbol*—The symbol of the two cups is worth contemplating today. If the angel pouring the liquid moved too hastily, the contents would spill out uncontrollably. This serves as a reminder that to achieve wellness and balance between body and mind, it's important to avoid extreme attitudes and temper strong passions with moderation.

HEALING

· *Today, the day ahead*—It's best to steer clear of anxieties, negative judgments, and pessimistic thoughts. Often, our perception of things can be clouded by a biased lens, causing us to see shadows where there are none.

· *Today, in love*—If your partner is feeling stressed, it's important not to withdraw. Instead, try offering small acts of affection to make them feel loved and supported. Consider writing a heartfelt message, preparing a soothing herbal tea, or offering a simple gesture that shows you care and want to be there for them.

· *Today, at work*—In the event of workplace conflicts, it may be incumbent upon you to diffuse the situation. Your presence will be invaluable, and your mediation skills could earn you appreciation and even advance your career.

· *Self-reflection*—Today is an ideal day for cleansing. Consider drinking herbal teas known for their purifying properties, opting for light and wholesome meals, and indulging in a clay mask while engaging in a calming or meditative activity. With this revitalizing routine, your body and mind will radiate positive energy.

· *A symbol*—The symbol worth reflecting on is the angel. Across many spiritual traditions, angels are regarded as celestial messengers and protectors. This Arcanum serves as a reminder that within each of us lies a higher guidance capable of leading us in the right direction, provided we know how to access it and listen attentively to it.

HARMONY

· *Today, the day ahead*—Have you noticed that everyone seems more friendly today, and that there's a sense of peace surrounding you? This isn't surprising, as starting your day with a smile can have a profound impact on your surroundings. The outcome of events reflects your approach to them.

· *Today, in love*—Whoever said that only grand and ostentatious gestures are the key to winning someone's heart? Sometimes, even amid the most ardent romances, simply being present, patient, and understanding is enough—without the need to prove or demand anything.

· *Today, at work*—Getting caught up in the hustle and bustle of work is pointless today. What you really need is calmness and precision. You'll discover that you have an abundance of expertise and concentration at your disposal. You may not be able to complete everything on your to-do list, but don't fret—patience is key, and at the very least, you'll have done your work with excellence.

· *Self-reflection*—Try not to impose too fast a pace on yourself if you can avoid it. Doing so might drain your energy and take a toll on your physical health. Take as much time as you need and consider seeking the advice of a reputable herbalist.

· *A symbol*—The symbol to reflect on is the triangle in the square, an ancient alchemical symbol that denotes the presence of divine essence in matter. Taking care of your physical body and treating it with love and respect will also nourish your soul.

Illusion · Servitude

The Devil card symbolizes your addictions and everything
that hinders your personal growth. It represents the obstacles
standing between you and your destiny.

Choose what kind of energy you want to draw from the Devil today:

Dependence, Obstacle, Materialism

DEPENDENCE

· *Today, the day ahead*—We all have our dependencies, whether small or large, in the form of habits or vices. However, emotional dependencies can be the most challenging to overcome. While today may not be the day to completely break the chains, you can take the first steps by loosening a few links and moving toward greater independence.

· *Today, in love*—It's easy to slip from a place of love to a place of dependency on your partner. Show them that you appreciate their presence, but also that you are capable of surviving without it. By doing so, your relationship will become healthier and more fulfilling. Remember that an obsessive need for a relationship can be a fixation that prevents you from making good choices, so it's important to break free from it.

· *Today, at work*—At work today, you may not have much leeway. Sometimes it's necessary to do what is asked of you. The time for creativity or rebellion will come eventually, just not right now.

· *Self-reflection*—Take a moment to reflect on the habits and negative thoughts that are deeply ingrained in you and seem impossible to let go of. Where do these dependencies come from? And how can you sever the bondage they have over you?

· *A symbol*—The symbol for today is the chains that bind the man and woman in the foreground, representing everything that impedes you from becoming who you're meant to be. Nevertheless, the chains aren't so tight that they cannot break free, indicating that the bond is subjective rather than objective.

OBSTACLE

· *Today, the day ahead*—Your value as an individual is not determined by your success but rather by the obstacles you overcome to achieve it. Life is not always easy, but your resilience in the face of adversity can make all the difference.

· *Today, in love*—Someone or something is standing in the way of a happy relationship. The sooner you identify who or what it is, the better.

· *Today, at work*—At times, no matter how much effort you put in, a competitor or rival may outdo you, sometimes through unfair means. On such days, all you can do is push yourself to prepare for the next challenge, confident in your abilities to perform better.

· *Self-reflection*—How can you identify and overcome the internal obstacles that hinder you the most? What is preventing you from being your authentic self and achieving your full potential?

· *A symbol*—Today's symbol is the lit torch. Your success would be meaningless without opposition, and your victories would hold no value without opponents. Even the obstacles in your path are something to be thankful for, as they provide opportunities for growth.

MATERIALISM

· *Today, the day ahead*—At times, the world can weigh you down with tasteless jokes, violent imagery, spiritual poverty, and degradation. Today it's important to rise above it all and not allow yourself to sink to the level of those you may encounter along the way.

· *Today, in love*—While it's important to address any issues in the realm of sex within a relationship, it's crucial to recognize that it cannot and should not be the sole foundation upon which the relationship is built. Focusing solely on the material aspect of a partnership will not provide a long-term solution.

· *Today, at work*—It's possible that an overly ambitious project may need to be scaled back and a goal might not be fully achieved. It's important not to let this discourage you. Remember, being able to handle failure or rejection with grace is also a valuable virtue.

· *Self-reflection*—Many of us devote a considerable amount of time and energy to meeting our basic needs, and while these needs are undoubtedly crucial, it's essential to bear in mind that life is not solely centered around fulfilling them. Set aside some time for interests that aren't solely materialistic and allow yourself to explore beyond the basic necessities of life.

· *A symbol*—The symbol to reflect on is the horns, which represent animalistic instinct that prevails over logic.

THE TOWER.

Manifestation · Collapse

This Arcanum represents a significant and transformative event that has
the power to shake things up from their very foundations. It signifies that
secrets and information that were previously kept under lock and key will be
revealed, and rigid structures will crumble. This, in turn, will create
openings and opportunities for a release of pent-up energy.

Choose what kind of energy you want to draw from the Tower today:
Warning, Liberation, Resolution

WARNING

· *Today, the day ahead*—Your life and daily plans may be unexpectedly disrupted by a sudden event, much like a bolt of lightning out of nowhere. It's important to accept and embrace this novelty with a sense of wonder and curiosity instead of succumbing to fear.

· *Today, in love*—Whether it caught you by surprise or was already in the air, Cupid's arrow has struck intensely! You can either choose to run away from it or you can allow yourself to be carried away by the intensity of its emotions. Either way, things will not be quite the same again.

· *Today, at work*—Having a sudden stroke of genius could be highly beneficial. If you come up with an idea, don't hesitate to jot it down, share it with others, propose it, or put it into action. This could greatly aid you in your work.

· *Self-reflection*—It's important to pay attention to the signals your body is sending you. Mind and body are intimately intertwined, meaning your mind can communicate through physical symptoms. When your mind is clear, your body tends to function better, so it's beneficial to listen to what your body is telling you.

· *A symbol*—The lightning strike symbolizes the sudden wake-up calls in life that bring us straight back down to earth. The thunderbolt that strikes the tower, knocking off its crown, serves as a reminder to stay grounded and not get too carried away.

LIBERATION

· *Today, the day ahead*—It's time to declutter and tidy up. Get rid of anything you no longer need and give your home and yourself a makeover if you have the time.

· *Today, in love*—If you are feeling overwhelmed and need to express your thoughts and feelings, do so in a way that is respectful and considerate of the people who care about you.

· *Today, at work*—Try to think outside of the box. Taking a calculated risk can help you reach a goal you have been striving for a long time. Remember, "No risk, no gain."

· *Self-reflection*—If you're feeling weighed down by old mental patterns and stuck in outdated behaviors, don't just accept them. Take steps to break free and follow your own path.

· *A symbol*—Today's symbol to reflect on is the explosion. When we accumulate too much, energy cannot flow, and life becomes complicated. This applies to physical objects, thoughts, and emotions alike.

RESOLUTION

· *Today, the day ahead*—It looks like a situation that has been stuck in limbo for a while could finally be resolved today, albeit causing some disruption to your daily routine. However, once done, the benefits will be unmistakable.

· *Today, in love*—A crisis can be a chance to reevaluate a relationship. If there is dissatisfaction, it's better to have an honest conversation and decide if the relationship is worth saving. It's time to take a step back, assess the situation, and determine whether putting the broken pieces back together is worth the effort or not.

· *Today, at work*—Today in the workplace, you may be seen as a bit of a revolutionary. While some may appreciate your efforts to bring transformation, others may struggle to accept it. Don't be discouraged; follow your intuition.

· *Self-reflection*—If you find yourself at a loss when it comes to solving a problem, take a step back and ask yourself whether it's worth starting from scratch. While it may feel daunting, the results will be worth it, and you'll be glad you took the time to do it right.

· *A symbol*—Today's symbol is the crown. Facing the unknown can be daunting, but it's the only way to take control of yourself and reach the top.

Future · Renewal · Destiny

Stars have always been a source of guidance and hope for mankind, showing us the way and reminding us to follow the laws of nature and the cosmos.

Choose what kind of energy you want to draw from the Star today:

Novelty, Possibility, Serenity

NOVELTY

· *Today, the day ahead*—The stars represent new beginnings, and the water poured by the young woman symbolizes rejuvenation. Today is a fantastic day to enthusiastically embrace the upcoming change.

· *Today, in love*—Something in your love life is about to change or has already changed. It might be time to infuse some excitement and change into your love life, so consider either shaking things up or getting ready for the arrival of a new experience.

· *Today, at work*—Don't be resistant to new experiences. Sometimes, making a change can help to break up a stagnant work situation and get things moving again.

· *Self-reflection*—Embrace changes with calmness and make them a part of your life. The stars are aligning in your favor today, asking you to trust in their guidance and have faith in what fate has in store for you.

· *A symbol*—The symbol for today is the eight-pointed star, Sirius. Just as it was once believed to signal the fertile inundation of the Nile, it now encourages you to prepare for good news and embrace whatever the future holds.

POSSIBILITY

· *Today, the day ahead*—There are multiple paths among the stars for you to explore, and it's important to have confidence in your ability to find the right one. With the right perspective, nothing is out of reach.

· *Today, in love*—Don't settle for less than you deserve. Strive for what serves you best and follow your inner compass.

· *Today, at work*—It's important to recognize that there may not be a single solution to a problem. Take the time to carefully consider various options before acting. Avoid acting impulsively and consider creating a plan to help you stay on the right course.

· *Self-reflection*—You have the power to be different versions of yourself, so ask yourself: who do you want to be today? Remember, who you were yesterday doesn't define who you are today or who you can become tomorrow.

· *A symbol*—Today's symbol is the ibis, a bird that represents prescience. With its flexible neck, it can look in any direction and explore all possibilities, leaving the final choice to intuition.

· *Today, the day ahead*—The sky is clear and full of stars, and the omens are in your favor. It seems like your problems are on the brink of being solved. To make the most of this opportunity, avoid being overwhelmed by anxiety and simply let things unfold naturally.

· *Today, in love*—If a choice makes you feel anxious, it's better to steer clear of it. Instead, go for the path that feels like the right one for you deep down.

· *Today, at work*—In the workplace, rushing is often unwise. It's better to take a moment to calmly analyze the situation. If you've fulfilled your commitments and done what's expected of you, there's no need to worry.

· *Self-reflection*—Let go of your worries and cultivate a sense of serenity in your mind. Starting your day with a calm and peaceful mindset can set the foundation for a successful day.

· *A symbol*—Reflect on the symbol of the woman pouring water, whose serene expression reflects the protection of the stars and assures you that you have nothing to fear.

THE MOON.

Intuition · Darkness

The Moon Arcanum connects you to the realm of the unconscious
and the feminine and receptive aspects of your character.
It's up to you to decide whether to fear them or channel them
toward a greater understanding of yourself.

Choose what kind of energy you want to draw from the Moon today:

Emotion, Indecision, Imagination

EMOTION

· *Today, the day ahead*—You may feel particularly sensitive. It's best to avoid situations that could cause anxiety or hurt your feelings.

· *Today, in love*—In matters of love, if you sense that your partner is acting different, try to communicate openly and ask them what's bothering them. It could be a worry or a fear that's upsetting them or just a bad dream.

· *Today, at work*—It's better not to rely too heavily on the help of others, as even small misunderstandings can cause major problems.

· *Self-reflection*—Are people opening to you and seeking your advice today? It's likely because your strong receptiveness is apparent to those around you. Be understanding and welcoming, as one day you may find yourself in need of someone to confide in.

· *A symbol*—Reflect on the symbol of the crab, a gentle creature that reminds us that beneath the toughest and most self-assured exteriors, there can often be a tender and fragile soul.

INDECISION

· *Today, the day ahead*—To solve a problem, don't just focus on the surface-level symptoms. Instead, dig deeper and search for the underlying causes, which will allow you to truly understand and address the issue. Only then will you be able to fully resolve the matter.

· *Today, in love*—Before making any hasty decisions, it's important to communicate with your partner and clarify any uncertainties. Sometimes a simple misunderstanding or oversight can lead to unwarranted anxiety and addressing it directly can help to dispel any baseless fears.

· *Today, at work*—Be sure to meticulously plan your strategy before starting any tasks. This can help you to efficiently manage your time and energy throughout the day, leading to greater productivity and success in the long run.

· *Self-reflection*—Do you hide parts of yourself from others because you fear they would make you seem vulnerable? What if those are the best aspects of your character that could help you shine if you only revealed them? Take some time to consider it.

· *A symbol*—The symbol to reflect on is the moon, which has two sides: one that we can see and the other that remains hidden. This serves as a reminder that everyone possesses a dual nature, even those who appear to have it all figured out, with admirable and respected qualities on one side, and less attractive ones on the other.

IMAGINATION

· *Today, the day ahead*—If you're feeling off today, don't push yourself. Taking some extra time to rest, relax at home, or browse through old photo albums can be therapeutic.

· *Today, in love*—To revive your relationship, consider starting a collaborative project, such as planning a trip or making a commitment together. Why not take the plunge and book that romantic cruise you've both always dreamed of? Don't delay any longer!

· *Today, at work*—Try to leave some space for your creativity and imagination. Allow yourself to experiment with new ideas and try things you've always wanted to but never had the chance. Not only could it be productive, it could also be an enjoyable experience.

· *Self-reflection*—Did a dream you had last night stick with you? Don't let it slip from your mind—jot down all the details and try to understand the message it's conveying. It could contain important insights that will help you in your everyday life.

· *A symbol*—Today, you can reflect on the symbol of the dog and the wolf. They represent the most primal and untamed aspects of our personality. While you may have tried to suppress them in the past, if you learn to embrace them, they can provide guidance and even protection in certain situations.

Vitality · Confidence · Freshness

The Sun is a symbol of vitality, spontaneity, and excitement in your life.
At a deeper level, it represents the moment of enlightenment
that can lead to a higher state of understanding.

Choose what kind of energy you want to draw from the Sun today:

Radiance, Honesty, Success

RADIANCE

· *Today, the day ahead*—Sharing positive energy with others can greatly enhance your day. A simple act of kindness like a friendly smile can be contagious and spread joy to those around you.

· *Today, in love*—Take time to observe your partner at their best and try to maintain or encourage that state of grace in your relationship. Doing so can bring great benefits to your relationship.

· *Today, at work*—Try to be outgoing and communicate your vision clearly. You may be surprised at how much easier it is to get people to follow your lead when you speak openly and confidently.

· *Self-reflection*—It's crucial to keep in mind that you are made of the same substance as the stars. This realization can be extremely illuminating and bring about transformative change.

· *A symbol*—The symbol for reflection today is the sun rays, which represent the light and warmth that accompany self-realization.

HONESTY

· *Today, the day ahead*— Using convoluted language isn't always necessary. Some days, it's appropriate to speak plainly and call a spade a spade.

· *Today, in love*—Having an open and honest conversation, where nothing is left unsaid or hidden, is a great way to begin addressing any issue.

· *Today, at work*—Stand behind your ideas with the power of simplicity, without being intimidated by the situation or individuals involved.

· *Self-reflection*—It is easy and effortless to deceive yourself, but it ultimately leads to dead ends. Therefore, it's important to take the time to reflect on the truths you may be avoiding about yourself or the world around you.

· *A symbol*—The symbol for reflection today is the child, representing the absence of filters, complete transparency, and sincerity.

SUCCESS

· *Today, the day ahead*—Everything seems to be aligned for something to go well, either for you or for someone close to you. If there is a day to take a risk, this is it.

· *Today, in love*—Today is an auspicious day for making plans with your partner, asking someone you're interested in out on a date, or feeling content in your romantic situation.

· *Today, at work*—The most fulfilling aspect of work is not necessarily the size of your paycheck. The sense of accomplishment that comes with a job well done, the admiration of a colleague, or the appreciation of a client can be more valuable than any salary increase. Regardless, today presents a prime opportunity to take advantage of and maximize your potential.

· *Self-reflection*—Having self-confidence is the key to succeeding in your projects. Believing in yourself and what you're doing is the first step toward achieving victory.

· *A symbol*—Today's symbol for reflection is the sunflower, representing optimism that paves the way for success.

Rebirth · Vocation

The Judgement card symbolizes triumphing over challenges
and discovering your true calling in life. It can also serve
as a motivating force for taking action and discovering yourself.

Choose what kind of energy you want to draw from the Judgement today:

Redemption, Vocation, Improvement

REDEMPTION

· *Today, the day ahead*—This might be the ideal day to declutter your cellar or attic. Who knows, you may stumble upon something you had once thought lost or even a cherished family heirloom.

· *Today, in love*— If you and your partner have been experiencing some challenges that have affected your sense of peace and tranquility, don't worry. Those issues will likely fade away, allowing the happiness and joy you once shared to take center stage once again. It appears that this will be a day filled with calmness and serenity.

· *Today, at work*—Finally, as if by sheer luck, you can take a deep breath and relax. You will likely be able to swiftly resolve complex issues that may have been hindering your progress or causing complications for some time now.

· *Self-reflection*—Consider reaching out to someone with whom you've lost touch. If you've been carrying feelings of guilt toward this person, it may be time to apologize and make amends. It may not be an easy task, but once done, the sense of relief and pride in yourself will make it all worthwhile.

· *A symbol*—Think about the symbol of the grave. The exposed tombs in this Arcanum are a poignant reminder that issues left unresolved can often find a way to resurface and must be addressed to finally find resolution.

VOCATION

· *Today, the day ahead*—There's a chance you may receive long-awaited news or a message that has the potential to alter the course of your future. Be sure to check your mail, phone, and email.

· *Today, in love*—Make the most of the strong connection with your partner and embark on an exciting and invigorating experience together. Consider attending a concert, going dancing, or visiting a club where live music is played.

· *Today, at work*—Momentous changes may be on the horizon at your workplace, affecting not only yourself but also your colleagues, should you have any. This is a pivotal moment for you to showcase your skills and prove your mettle.

· *Self-reflection*—It's time to make a crucial decision, one that cannot be postponed any further. It may not be easy with multiple responsibilities to shoulder but trust your instincts to lead you down the right path.

· *A symbol*—The symbol to reflect on today is the trumpet, which symbolizes your calling—the clarion call to express your true essence, talents, or life mission.

IMPROVEMENT

· *Today, the day ahead*—The dream that you have always longed for but never dared to hope for may finally become a reality. If a proposal arrives, do not hesitate to seize the opportunity and accept it.

· *Today, in love*—This is a particularly auspicious day for love: misunderstandings can be resolved, couples can rekindle their passion, and new romantic prospects may be on the horizon for those still seeking their soulmate.

· *Today, at work*—It's time to take a step back at work, evaluate what's working and what's not, and make necessary changes. Streamline processes, eliminate inefficiencies, and focus on areas that lead to growth and success. You may even find opportunities for career advancement.

· *Self-reflection*—Consider shedding old habits or patterns that no longer serve you. While it may be difficult for others to understand your transformation, do not be afraid to make changes and trust your intuition. Forge your own path and embrace new ways of being.

· *A symbol*—Reflect on the symbolism of the flag. While it typically represents a nation or ideal, on a personal level it can symbolize a deep identification with your own moral principles and values.

Completeness · Totality · Redemption

The World card signifies the end of a journey, the achievement of a goal, and the conclusion of a cycle. It is a card that signifies fulfillment but also carries the risk of becoming too complacent in your accomplishments.

Choose what kind of energy you want to draw from the World today:

Joy, Achievement, Rebirth

JOY

· *Today, the day ahead*—Every day has the potential to hold both small and grand moments of joy. It's crucial to seize these opportunities, savor them, and not let the weight of daily routine keep you from appreciating a smile, a sunset, or a kind gesture.

· *Today, in love*—Life is full of reasons to celebrate—from the first time you felt a deep connection, to the milestones you've reached together, to the fulfillment of shared aspirations. Make sure to take time to rejoice and celebrate these moments together!

· *Today, at work*—Although it may not be obvious to you, you are exactly where you are meant to be at this time.

· *Self-reflection*—Take some time to celebrate something you excel at, something that fills you with pride.

· *A symbol*—Consider the dancer, which symbolizes the importance of showing your inner happiness to the world around you. By doing so, you can invite others to join in and add to that joy.

ACHIEVEMENT

· *Today, the day ahead*—While the journey itself holds significance, the destination it leads to is equally important. Today presents an opportunity to bring your journey to a fitting conclusion.

· *Today, in love*—You have achieved your goal, and your path has reached its destination. Take a moment to reflect on your journey before choosing a new goal and embarking on a new path.

· *Today, at work*—It's easy to feel overwhelmed by criticism, but it's important not to lose sight of your accomplishments. Take some time to reflect on what you've achieved and all that you've succeeded in accomplishing, rather than getting caught up in what's still left to do or what's expected of you.

· *Self-reflection*—The road to self-improvement never truly ends, but it's important to take a moment today to reflect on the progress you've already made. Consider the obstacles you've overcome and the successes you've achieved thus far.

· *A symbol*—Consider reflecting on the symbol of the laurel wreath today. It represents the rightful recognition and reward for hard work, the fulfillment of a long-awaited desire, and the eternal glory of one's achievements.

· *Today, the day ahead*—Today is the day to shed the burdens of the past, to bring closure to a thought, a project, or a cycle, and prepare to start anew unencumbered by what has weighed you down thus far.

· *Today, in love*—It's time to put an end to an argument, let go of any grudges, and seek or offer forgiveness. Mistakes have been recognized, and amends have been made. A fresh start is in the cards.

· *Today, at work*—Today may present a valuable opportunity to rectify past mistakes, overcome shortcomings, and bring closure to ongoing matters in a peaceful and satisfactory manner. This can pave the way for a fresh start and prepare new endeavors.

· *Self-reflection*—To purify your soul and create a better version of yourself, it's important to leave behind your flaws. Shedding the things that weigh you down on your journey, cleansing the soul, are essential steps toward regeneration.

· *A symbol*—Today's symbol for reflection, offered by the World, is the elliptical shape of the laurel wreath. This shape represents the archway symbolizing the birth or rebirth of the soul of the earth and embodies the immense power of creative energy.

Fullness · Contemplation

The Ace of Cups symbolizes the Grail, which is believed
to be the source of spiritual rejuvenation. This card serves as a symbol
of protection, indicating that happiness, satisfaction, creativity,
and important emotions are on the horizon.

Choose what kind of energy you want to draw from the Ace of Cups today:

Love, Creativity, Abundance

LOVE

· *Today, the day ahead*—Today may be the day when something unexpected yet long-awaited arrives. Don't close yourself off to emotions and feelings, as the cup is overflowing with good news.

· *Today, in love*—In matters of love, the energy between you and your partner will be unique and intense. You will experience the proverbial butterflies in your stomach and the joy of finally finding that special someone.

· *Today, at work*—It's a good time to lend a helping hand to others. You'll discover that the more you give, the more you receive.

· *Self-reflection*—You have the power to prevent negative emotions from taking over and the ability to forgive someone, even yourself. Let go of anger and find inner peace.

 · *A symbol*—Consider the symbol of the hand, which represents offering a benevolent and strong hand that can bring love and abundance. What you give will be returned to you with the same intensity. Reach out to others with confidence, offering the best of yourself, and you'll find others who will help you when you need it most.

CREATIVITY

· *Today, the day ahead*—Today is a very special day, as the forces of heaven seem to be on your side, bringing together a powerful creative energy inside of you. This could be the beginning of something new—whether it's a business venture or the birth of a child.

· *Today, in love*—You are extremely open to your inner feelings and are eager to share them with others. You could even channel this deep sense of empathy into your art, allowing others to see the world through your eyes and feel your overflowing emotions.

· *Today, at work*—You might feel inspired to start a new creative project or sign up for an art or dance class. You have already poured a lot of your fertile energy and love into a design idea, and now is the time to bring it to life.

· *Self-reflection*—You are feeling confident and at peace with your emotional side. By expressing your emotions in a constructive way, you will gain a more balanced perspective and strength in all areas of your life.

· *A symbol*—The symbol to meditate on today is the dove, which symbolizes the embodiment of spirit in the material world. By channeling your emotional universe in the right way, you can give physical form to your projects and ideas, making your soul light and your heart filled with a strong sense of satisfaction and peace.

ABUNDANCE

· *Today, the day ahead*—Today is the perfect day to live fully and with satisfaction. Whether you choose to stay at home or go out, you can enjoy every moment with joy. With overflowing energy, you will be able to experience intense positive emotions.

· *Today, in love*—You will be an overflowing cup of love and generously offer yourself to your loved ones. No matter how much they drink, you will not feel emptied of love, but rather even more abundant. The joy you can give and the beauty around you will fill your soul.

· *Today, at work*—At work, your soul is in a creative ferment! Satisfaction is on the horizon, as your proactivity and birth of new ideas may lead to promotions. You are like a river in full flow, and all your efforts will be rewarded abundantly.

· *Self-reflection*—You have a thousand overlapping ideas and an infinite desire to do and give. It would be a shame not to take advantage of such a propitious moment, wouldn't it? Take a walk outdoors and let yourself be permeated by the beauty around you.

· *A symbol*—Today's symbol to contemplate is the cup. It's important to approach life with an open and welcoming attitude to fully experience all it has to offer. If you keep yourself closed off, you won't be able to appreciate the many gifts that life tries to bestow upon you. Don't wait until you feel completely ready—take a leap of faith and watch as prosperity and wealth flood into your life.

Encounter · Union

The Two of Cups signifies the start of an emotional and spiritual connection, where two individuals come together to form a bond of harmony.
It represents the transformation from "I" to "us," making it a positive card not only for those seeking love or friendship but also for those pursuing a shared group project based on similar values and interests.

Choose what kind of energy you want to draw from the Two of Cups today:

Encounter, Love Union, Friendship

ENCOUNTER

· *Today, the day ahead*—Don't let your past wounds hold you back from opening to the people you encounter on your journey. Trust is a precious gift, and today you might meet someone who truly values it.

· *Today, in love*—Experiencing a profound connection, mutual understanding, and love between two individuals is not limited to fairy tales portrayed by Disney. It could be a reality for you if you are open to seizing the opportunities that come your way.

· *Today, at work*—Let go of any tension that has built up. You might start new collaborations that are long-lasting, or a colleague with whom you work well could return to your professional circle after a temporary absence.

· *Self-reflection*—Sometimes when we look in the mirror, we don't like what we see, and we may even feel as though we're looking at a stranger. However, it's important to confront and accept our true selves to better understand others and cultivate mutually harmonious relationships.

· *A symbol*—Consider the symbolism of the two cups. Each cup is filled with its own unique essence and has its own identity. When they are brought together, they have the potential to grow and become something greater than themselves.

LOVE UNION

· *Today, the day ahead*—Rekindle your love for yourself, those around you, the things you love doing, and the environment you inhabit. As you do so, you'll experience a profound sense of harmony flowing through you, akin to a river in full flood, sweeping away any doubts or uncertainties. Today is an opportune moment to embrace love with love.

· *Today, in love*—A mutual attraction between two people may develop into a romantic relationship. You both feel a special connection, but it's ultimately up to you to determine if this bond can transform into a lasting union. The foundation is solid and promising, but it's important that both parties are willing to put in the effort and commitment necessary for a successful relationship.

· *Today, at work*—In the workplace, you may have the support and appreciation of someone close to you—perhaps a friend or family member—who believes in you wholeheartedly and knows how to help you reach your full potential. This person can be instrumental in fostering productive collaborations and bringing out the best in you.

· *Self-reflection*—Today, begin anew with yourself: love yourself and cultivate a loving relationship with yourself and the life you are constructing each day, amid setbacks and triumphs. Love yourself without conceit, acknowledging the worth of all your mistakes. You will discover a sense of harmony that you can transmit to the partnership you are already in or the one you will have in the future.

· *A symbol*—Today's symbol for reflection is the lion's head. It symbolizes the strength within a relationship between two individuals, a strength of emotions and intentions. To transition from attraction to love, it's essential to have a strong desire for the well-being of the other, even more than one's own, and this must be reciprocated to establish a harmonious balance.

FRIENDSHIP

· *Today, the day ahead*—Real friendship is all about giving and taking in a mutually selfless and balanced exchange that stands the test of time. Surround yourself with these precious gems and be thankful and open to making space for the friendships you come across on your journey.

· *Today, in love*—Friendship is a form of love that involves trusting and being sincere with others, and it can develop between individuals of the same or different species. Sometimes, words are not needed to understand this type of bond—you can simply look into the eyes of your pet and feel the warmth of a genuine and selfless friendship.

· *Today, at work*—Whether it's a collaboration or a partnership, you will embark on a new project with like-minded and motivated companions who share many similarities with you.

· *Self-reflection*—If your heart tells you that you're not on equal terms in a relationship, and you feel drained of all your energy, despite making several attempts at dialogue that have only left you feeling guilty and uncomfortable, then it might be time to reconsider and redefine that friendship.

· *A symbol*—Today, you can reflect on the caduceus of Mercury. To develop a relationship based on reciprocity and balance, it's essential to find a common ground with the other person. This requires effort, willpower, and wisdom, but it's through this type of commitment that you can build a healthy and lasting relationship over time.

Festivity · The Third Wheel

The Three of Cups card represents celebration and fulfillment, with happiness, abundance, and a sense of satisfaction from victories achieved. Although there may be challenges and obstacles to come, with perseverance and determination you can still attain what you desire.

Choose what kind of energy you want to draw from the Three of Cups today:
Prosperity, Birth, Festivity

PROSPERITY

· *Today, the day ahead*—You're currently experiencing a period of flourishing growth where you feel great both physically and emotionally, and you can handle any minor challenges that come your way with ease.

· *Today, in love*—This is a fantastic opportunity to let loose a little and revel in the harmony of your family, the support of your friends, and the love that's blooming within you. It's the perfect moment to spend quality time with those who matter most to you.

· *Today, at work*—You have the chance to reap the rewards of the dedication and selflessness exhibited by you and your closely knit team, as you witness your earnings and business grow in terms of profit.

· *Self-reflection*—Take pleasure in this moment of grace, satisfaction, and serenity that comes with a job well done and skillfully managed interpersonal relationships. It's likely the moment you've been waiting for all your life, so relish in all the gifts this abundant cornucopia has to offer.

· *A symbol*—Today, you can reflect on the symbols of flowers and fruits, which represent the beauty that surrounds us if we only take the time to appreciate it. Simply reach out and harvest the abundance of gifts that this moment of grace offers you and breathe in the scent of a luxuriously opulent cornucopia.

BIRTH

· *Today, the day ahead*—Embrace the opportunity to reap the rewards of your inner journey today. As you synthesize your desires and reconcile your inner conflicts, a newfound harmony will emerge, giving birth to a world of creative possibilities and long-awaited accomplishments. Get ready to taste the sweetest fruit of your labor and enjoy the journey toward a fulfilling life project.

· *Today, in love*—You're in a relationship where you feel perfectly harmonious with your partner, and you both happily complement each other. It's that beautiful and rare type of love that creates all kinds of opportunities. You may even consider getting married or be thrilled by the news of a successful pregnancy or adoption.

· *Today, at work*—Collaborating with your colleagues and sharing your creative energy and passion can lead to great achievements. You may even see the birth of a new and promising project.

· *Self-reflection*—You may sense a tremendous creative energy blossoming inside you, waiting to be expressed and given form. Don't let the conformity of those around you stifle this fortunate novelty that's emerging within you. Let it bloom in all its beauty and perfection.

· *A symbol*—Today's symbol to contemplate is the three women as creative forces, givers of life, and sources of fertility. Their dance recalls the three Graces in Botticelli's *Primavera*. It's a reminder that everything is geared toward rebirth and new beginnings as life awakens once again.

FESTIVITY

· *Today, the day ahead*—Remember that life should be celebrated at every moment because it's a gift! At this specific moment, something long awaited may happen that will bring you overwhelming joy, and it should be celebrated with your friends and loved ones.

· *Today, in love*—Whether it's an important anniversary, a wedding, an engagement, or a first date, cherish and celebrate it, as it will be a moment that you'll hold dear to your heart for years to come.

· *Today, at work*—You have finally accomplished a significant goal that you have been working toward. You may feel tired but also satisfied and fulfilled with both your work and that of your team. It is time to share the joy of your success!

· *Self-reflection*—Your heart is filled with joy. Take time to savor every moment and celebrate the small and big things that everyday life has to offer.

· *A symbol*—Today's symbol for contemplation is the three cups raised to the sky, which represents a toast to joy and accomplished goals. It's also a moment of sharing that joy with loved ones or colleagues. This is a gesture of gratitude toward the benevolent fate that brought you together, because no joy is complete without someone to share it with.

Material Comfort · Boredom

The Four of Cups represents a person who has everything
they need materially, but still feels dissatisfied. It signifies a need
to reflect on yourself to find what can give you genuine enthusiasm
for life without being distracted by trivial matters.

Choose what kind of energy you want to draw from the Four of Cups today:

Stability, Dissatisfaction, Opportunity

STABILITY

· *Today, the day ahead*—You are currently in a stable and secure situation, but this may cause you to feel a slight sense of lethargy toward the beauty that surrounds you and the opportunities that come your way. Taking what you have for granted could lead to the risk of losing it.

· *Today, in love*—There is plenty of love in your life: appreciate it and give it the value it deserves, otherwise, you may miss out on the opportunity to enjoy it. Reconnect with others and let them know how much you appreciate them.

· *Today, at work*—Days are passing by peacefully, one after the other. You are approaching your work with your usual confidence, yet a subtle restlessness is brewing within you that you can't seem to shake off but are too afraid to face. Take a step back and reflect.

· *Self-reflection*—Looking around, you'll realize that you have nothing to complain about; your life is progressing well on the path you have chosen. However, this apparent state of stability and firmness may work against you at times because you might miss out on new relationships, opportunities, and other significant aspects of your life.

· *A symbol*—Today, take a moment to contemplate the symbol of the three cups. Everything beautiful and valuable that you have created in your life is right in front of you. Don't just admire it like a painting or let it carry you away like the current of a river. It belongs to you! Embrace it and cherish it.

DISSATISFACTION

· *Today, the day ahead*—At a critical moment, you may experience feelings of apathy or demotivation. Life can seem monotonous and unexciting, lacking the necessary spark to push you forward. Activities that once brought joy may now appear irrelevant, leaving you unable to fully appreciate what you have. At the same time, you may struggle to find the courage to make the necessary changes in your life.

· *Today, in love*—You might be feeling stuck in a relationship that no longer feels like your own, but you continue to hold on to it without making any changes. It's unclear whether you're doing this because you genuinely care about your partner or simply out of habit.

· *Today, at work*—You may find yourself feeling fatigued at work. The goals you've accomplished in the past no longer bring you satisfaction, and the once comforting work routine is now slowly causing frustration, even though there isn't anything tangible to blame for this feeling. It's important to look within yourself to identify what is causing this unease and where you can make improvements.

· *Self-reflection*—You might be experiencing a phase of stagnation, boredom, or apathy, and it's understandable to feel restless and eager to move past it. Instead of dwelling on negative thoughts and unhelpful behaviors, try to connect with others and show them your appreciation. Doing so can help to rejuvenate your spirit and provide a much-needed source of renewal.

· *A symbol*—As a symbol to reflect on during this time, consider the image of the man sitting under a tree. This figure appears deep in thought, seemingly disinterested in everything around him. Despite being motionless and firmly rooted to the ground, his gaze is directed downward rather than upward toward the leaves and sky above.

OPPORTUNITY

· *Today, the day ahead*—It's time to snap out of your daze and seize the moment. A wonderful opportunity is just around the corner, but if you hesitate and fail to take action, you may watch it slip away right before your eyes. Remember the phrase "Carpe diem!" and make the most of every opportunity that comes your way.

· *Today, in love*—If you're currently in a romantic relationship, pay attention to the signs the universe is sending your way and be open to new experiences. Sometimes life has a way of placing the right person in our path at just the right moment, but it's up to us to have the courage to recognize it and take a chance.

· *Today, at work*—Consider the opportunities you may be overlooking at work and ask yourself whether this is due to a lack of confidence in your ability to benefit from them, or if fear is holding you back. Be mindful of any defensive reactions or attitudes that may arise.

· *Self-reflection*—If you come across a promising opportunity but don't feel ready to make a decision, it's important to take some time to reflect and gain clarity. Once you feel emotionally prepared and have gathered all the necessary information, you'll be better equipped to make a well-informed choice about whether to accept the opportunity or not.

· *A symbol*—Today, the symbol to contemplate is the offered cup. You've been presented with an opportunity, but you may be delaying your decision-making and evaluation, leaving everything in a state of uncertainty until you've cleared your mind.

FIVE OF CUPS

Sadness · Forgiveness

The Five of Cups symbolizes a challenging situation
that can create a deep sense of sadness and oppression. It's crucial
to keep in mind that just because you may not currently see a solution,
it doesn't mean that there isn't one out there.

Choose what kind of energy you want to draw from the Five of Cups today:

Sorrow, Change, Forgiveness

SORROW

· *Today, the day ahead*—If you're feeling disillusioned with life and weighed down by a deep sadness that, has you fixated on the "glass half full," don't let bitterness consume you and trap your emotions and relationships. Instead, remember that every experience—even painful ones—can open the door to inner growth.

· *Today, in love*—It seems like you're still caught up in the past, constantly mulling over memories and actions that have left you feeling regretful and bitter. You might be disappointed in yourself or someone else. Take some time to reflect on what happened and work toward finding inner peace. Give yourself the space you need to process your thoughts and emotions.

· *Today, at work*— As the old saying goes, "When one door closes, another one opens," and this is especially true when it comes to work. It's understandable to feel upset and confused when something you've been counting on, like a job opportunity or a project, doesn't pan out. However, it's important not to get too caught up in what's been taken away from you.

· *Self-reflection*—Instead of letting pessimism take over, try to focus on the opportunities still available to you. It's easy to fall into the trap of thinking that you'll never emerge from this feeling of sadness, but that's simply not true. Take some time to reflect on your strengths and what you hope to achieve in the future. With perseverance and hard work, there's no limit to what you can accomplish.

· *A symbol*—Today, reflect on the symbol of the black cloak. It's a representation of negative emotions that can take over if you let them. It might feel like a cozy cocoon that you can retreat to, where your sadness is cushioned and bearable. However, this is a false sense of comfort.

CHANGE

· *Today, the day ahead*—After experiencing regret, nostalgia, and sadness, you can look forward to a future filled with hope. You've realized that this difficult experience has been a learning opportunity, and you've gained valuable lessons from it.

· *Today, in love*—When it comes to your love life, you're now prepared to release the pain from your past and transition into a new chapter. This fresh start brings with it exciting opportunities, such as new relationships, interests, and emotional experiences that you've yet to encounter.

· *Today, at work*— In your career life, you've reached a point where you're able to release the burden of tasks or jobs that have been causing you undue stress, frustration, and sadness. Now you're prepared to welcome new opportunities that will bring you a sense of fulfillment and happiness.

· *Self-reflection*—You're beginning to break free from a victim mentality and acknowledge the significance of confronting disappointments as a means to discover what genuinely matters in life.

· *A symbol*—Today's symbol is the bridge, which signifies our capacity to surmount obstacles and form meaningful connections with others and different aspects of ourselves. It serves as a reminder that we, as humans, possess the ability to construct bridges and triumph over the agonizing states of loneliness and disconnection.

FORGIVENESS

· *Today, the day ahead*—It's important to let go of the past and allow it to flow away with the passage of time. Dwelling on it with regret or constantly revisiting it in your memories won't do you any good. Instead, learn to forgive yourself and accept that the past is just one piece of your life.

· *Today, in love*—In love, misunderstandings and hurt are bound to happen, but they don't always have to result in a relationship crisis. Understanding is crucial in all forms of love, so it's important to pay attention to each other's words, wounds, and needs. Reflect on them with a clear mind, setting aside anger, disappointment, and pride. Finally, communicate with each other using mutual understanding.

· *Today, at work*—Reflecting on past experiences at work can provide valuable lessons, even when things don't go according to plan.

· *Self-reflection*—Rather than succumbing to pessimism and guilt, it's important to examine the facts with clarity and reflect on them to facilitate personal growth and evolution.

· *A symbol*—Today's symbol is the river. Its clear waters wash away impurities and smooth out rough surfaces, while also nourishing and sustaining life on its unceasing journey toward its destination. Just like a river does, allow time to wash away any negativity and help propel you toward your own goals.

Harmony · Memories

The Six of Cups symbolizes gentleness and innocence,
a balance between the pleasant memories of the past and the hopefulness
of the future—all of which can be experienced in the present by savoring
the little joys of life and simple, pure connections with others.

Choose what kind of energy you want to draw from the Six of Cups today:

Harmony, Memories, Fulfilled Wishes

HARMONY

· *Today, the day ahead*—By bringing the positive energy from your past into your present, you can positively influence your future. Although the present and future may seem disconnected, they impact each other in the present moment. There's no need for conflict between the various seasons of life.

· *Today, in love*—Take a moment to observe children: to them, the world is a perfect place filled with endless possibilities to experience and rejoice with absolute trust. As you observe, you'll begin to realize that your heart too can be open and innocent like theirs, ready to embrace the past with all its memories, the present with all its blessings, and the future with its wonderful opportunities.

· *Today, at work*—You have achieved a solid balance at work, both internally and in your relationships with colleagues. You confidently share your talents with them without worrying about their opinions or judgments. You're secure in your value and the choices you're making in the present.

· *Self-reflection*—It's time to stop dwelling on the past and living with regrets. Instead, it's time to fully embrace the present moment. When you find yourself in this state of grace—feeling spontaneous, creative, and intuitive—and when you allow yourself to be your genuine, authentic self, that's when you can truly discover what lies deep within you.

· *A symbol*—Today, let's reflect on the symbol of 'children.' Sometimes, to find peace and let go of the burdens in our lives, we need to reconnect with our true essence—our most innocent and pure selves.

MEMORIES

· *Today, the day ahead*—Today, you may find yourself reminiscing about memories from your past—moments in your life to which you are emotionally attached. You'll likely feel a mix of tenderness and nostalgia, and you may even be tempted to retreat into those memories. But remember, you are no longer the same person you were then. You've gained experience and grown in wisdom. Instead of wallowing in the past, let those memories serve as inspiration to live fully in the present.

· *Today, in love*—You may feel a strong urge to revisit a place from your childhood or a familiar setting from your past. You might even reconnect with an old flame from your adolescent years, with whom you can reminisce about the good times you shared in a peaceful and serene manner.

· *Today, at work*—At work, you're moving beyond past assumptions. You may reference the past, but you're focused on the future and what's new. Any past conflicts related to everyday professional life have gradually been resolved with the passage of time.

· *Self-reflection*—While it's important to explore memories of the past, it's crucial not to idealize them and get stuck in them. The past is a part of you, but it's behind you. Take a comprehensive look at your past—not only the beauty of innocence, but also the difficulties, disappointments, and challenges that helped shape who you are today.

· *A symbol*—Today's symbol for reflection is the older man walking away. This image symbolizes the worries and conflicts you've faced head-on, which may have caused you pain but ultimately helped you grow. As these struggles fade away in the distance, they offer you the chance to find peace and innocence in your memories.

FULFILLED WISHES

· *Today, the day ahead*—You will realize that everything you have sown and fought for in the past has finally blossomed and is ready for you to enjoy. You will be amazed at the simplicity with which it is offered to you, and the delicate strength with which it is revealed to you. You have earned it, and it will last.

· *Today, in love*—You may experience the blossoming of a simple and pure love, much like that of a child. It could be the birth or adoption of a child, or you may simply find joy in spending more time with your children, playing, laughing, and growing together.

· *Today, at work*—You will have the strength and energy to handle any new changes that come your way. You've learned to see things from a fresh perspective and, by making the right choices, you're achieving the goals and rewards you have aimed for.

· *Self-reflection*—You feel as though your soul has been cleansed of all ugliness and worries, and a pervasive sense of joy is filling your being. This joy will draw an abundance of gifts into your life, both hoped for and unexpected, with a magnetic attraction.

· *A symbol*—Today's symbol to reflect on is the cup filled with flowers. Behold the fruits of your tireless labor, transformed into wondrous blessings that will endure the test of time and never lose their luster. This symbol evokes the feeling of being reborn into a new season of your life.

Choice · Illusion

The Seven of Cups represents an individual whose attention is caught up
in a thousand dreams and goals, the value of which, however, remains
doubtful even when they are realized. You must choose your steps carefully,
otherwise you run the risk of dissipating your energy in hazy projects.

Choose what kind of energy you want to draw from the Seven of Cups today:
Choice, Illusion, Surprise

CHOICE

· *Today, the day ahead*—You have been given the opportunity to turn your dreams into reality, but it's important to prioritize and focus your energy on the ones that truly matter. Otherwise, you risk wasting your efforts on pursuits that may not lead to anything significant.

· *Today, in love*—When it comes to love, take the time to think about what matters most to you, what you want out of life, and the kind of partner you want by your side; then make your decisions based on that.

· *Today, at work*—When it comes to work, it's important to be mindful of the decisions you make, considering the advantages and disadvantages of each option. Don't be fooled by initial impressions; there's often more than meets the eye.

· *Self-reflection*—Stop daydreaming and start taking action to make your dreams a reality. Don't be overwhelmed by all the possibilities, just make sure you make the right choices.

· *A symbol*—The symbol you can reflect on today is the cups filled with gifts. Everything you have wished for or hoped to achieve at different points in your life may suddenly become available to you, either through luck or an opportunity, and you may feel overwhelmed and confused. Think about which of those desires no longer fit with who you are now, and you will be able to make the right decision.

ILLUSION

· *Today, the day ahead*—You may not know what it would take for you to feel truly fulfilled, as you have many aspirations. However, the beliefs you have about your life may be based on false assumptions. It's essential to differentiate between what is real and what is just an illusion.

· *Today, in love*— Perhaps you have put someone on a pedestal, only seeing the parts of them that fit with what you want and ignoring the rest. Love means accepting them for who they are, flaws and all.

· *Today, at work*—If you want to reach your goals and fulfill your dreams, you need to be able to recognize the reality of the situation at work. Don't waste your time and energy on projects that are impossible to achieve.

· *Self-reflection*—If you don't stay grounded, you won't be able to make your dreams come true or conquer your fears. You need to learn to face the realities of life with determination and strength. Don't let yourself be consumed by fantasies and worries—that won't get you anywhere.

· *A symbol*—Take a moment to reflect on the symbol of the cloud. Clouds can evoke both feelings of joy and sadness as they remind us of the fleeting nature of things and the evanescence of dreams. Yet, they can also bring us joy with their beauty.

SURPRISE

· *Today, the day ahead*—You may be surprised by the many unexpected opportunities that come your way, leaving you feeling overwhelmed and unable to decide which one is best for you. Take time to reflect and you will be rewarded with the right choice.

· *Today, in love*—If someone suddenly and unexpectedly opened their soul to you, you could be taken aback by the multitude of complexities and nuances present. This is a beautiful gesture of trust, but it also comes with a great deal of responsibility.

· *Today, at work*—Your talents have been recognized without needing to be flaunted. You've been asked to take on multiple tasks at once, which is both flattering and intimidating. It's a double-edged sword—you can't spread yourself too thin and expect to do your best in each task.

· *Self-reflection*—Who am I? What do I want? Where am I heading? These are all questions that can be overwhelming, but the answers can be found within. Take some time to reflect on yourself and you will be amazed at what you can discover. Don't be afraid to accept all aspects of yourself, even the flaws you may have been denying. By doing this, you will find the answers you seek.

· *A symbol*—Today, take some time to reflect on the symbolism of the man seen from behind. His arm is raised in surprise, serving as a reminder that life can bring us unexpected situations, difficult decisions, and opportunities to choose from. It can be intimidating, but if you let fear take control, you won't be able to progress and grow.

Change · Journey

The Eight of Cups is a card of transformation and transition. It's time
to move on from a familiar but no longer fulfilling lifestyle and embark
on a new journey in pursuit of greater ambitions, even in a spiritual sense.

Choose what kind of energy you want to draw from the Eight of Cups today:
Change, Journey, Abandonment

CHANGE

· *Today, the day ahead*—Now that you've accomplished your goals, you find that the satisfaction you expected is not quite there, leaving you feeling unsettled. There's no material item that can fix this inner turmoil; you must start from within your soul to find the true treasure that will bring you the balance you seek.

· *Today, in love*—You may feel like you've put in a lot of effort with little to show for it, but this is the perfect opportunity for an emotional reset. By ending this relationship, you can open the door to new possibilities in the future.

· *Today, at work*—If you're feeling stuck in a rut at work, don't worry—something exciting is coming soon!

· *Self-reflection*—You feel the urge to venture into uncharted territories and discover new opportunities, but you're afraid of missing out on the benefits of your current situation. Taking risks is always a gamble, but if the alternative is to remain stagnant and uninspired, then it's worth taking a calculated risk.

· *A symbol*—Today's symbol to contemplate is the eclipse. It indicates the completion of a lunar and solar cycle that has always held great significance for humanity's existence on this planet. The conclusion of one cycle always marks the start of another, both of which are part of a continuous and eternal flow.

JOURNEY

· *Today, the day ahead*—Having lived fully and achieved great successes, there's no better time than now to take a step back from the rat race and embark on a journey of self-discovery, while pursuing deep spiritual goals.

· *Today, in love*—You may consider a move for sentimental reasons; you're not afraid of any challenges that may come up and you're confident that you can handle them because the potential benefits are worth it.

· *Today, at work*—You'll have excellent opportunities for improvement at work if you learn to act in new ways. With this understanding, you may choose to pursue a training course, collaborating with companies (including those abroad) in fields related to or useful for your own.

· *Self-reflection*—You may feel that it's time to begin an introspective journey—an experience of active meditation—with the aim of revitalizing your productivity and enthusiasm.

· *A symbol*—Today, the symbols to reflect on are the cloak and the red shoes. Your courage is unwavering and wraps around you like a cloak, giving you the confidence to take decisive steps forward. Driven by your inner restlessness and attraction to the unknown, you're not afraid to let go of what you know and embark on a solitary journey within yourself, navigating life's uncertainties along the way.

ABANDONMENT

· *Today, the day ahead*—The treasures that once dazzled and motivated you now seem completely insignificant. You're in search of a greater truth, and you're willing to leave behind past relationships, achievements, and projects. You've realized that happiness is not about being surrounded by luxury, fleeting friends, or casual lovers. True happiness is being at peace with your thoughts and feelings and staying true to yourself.

· *Today, in love*—You've given so much, and committed yourself emotionally to the point of feeling drained. You feel like the only option left is to walk away from this situation. While it's a bitter pill to swallow, you know it's the right decision to avoid burning out entirely.

· *Today, at work*—You may be at a point in your career where you feel like giving up, as the daily frustrations can be draining. It's a good time to take a break and focus on building up your self-confidence.

· *Self-reflection*—Escaping from your problems won't make them disappear. Pay attention to all the warning signs your body is sending you. If you need a medical checkup or just need to take a break from the hectic pace of work or your chaotic life, it's crucial you do so as soon as possible.

· *A symbol*—Today's symbol for contemplation is the man walking away. It can be hard to leave something unfinished, but you realize it's necessary right now. While there may be reluctance and doubt, facing these fears head-on can help you avoid getting trapped in a negative cycle that holds you back from achieving your full potential.

Wellness · Fulfillment

The Nine of Cups is generally considered to be auspicious. It suggests that you should have confidence in the projects you're pursuing, while also feeling grateful for what you already have. You should take pride in your achievements and feel fulfilled, knowing that you fully deserve them.

Choose what kind of energy you want to draw from the Nine of Cups today:
Fulfillment, Success, Self-Esteem

FULFILLMENT

· *Today, the day ahead*—The experiences and challenges you have faced, as well as the new relationships you've formed, have given you valuable wisdom and insight. This has allowed you to turn your dreams into a successful reality that you can now relish without fear or concern, and that you can share with others.

· *Today, in love*—You feel fulfilled and emotionally stable; your relationship is growing stronger every day and meeting your expectations.

· *Today, at work*—It is certainly true that modesty is a virtue, but today is a day to take pride in your hard work and self-sacrifice that have led to your achievements at work. Let your satisfaction and joy show, as your happiness can serve as an inspiration to others.

· *Self-reflection*—It's time to enjoy the present and be content with all the good things and beauty you have created in your life. You have achieved true happiness, a balanced and stable state of mind that you know can last over time. You're grateful for every life opportunity—both positive and negative—that has brought you to this moment.

· *A symbol*—Today's symbol for contemplation is the cups. It's important to take pleasure in both your material and spiritual accomplishments, as they represent the fulfillment of your deepest aspirations. Take in the beauty around you and allow yourself to fully experience the joy that comes with it.

SUCCESS

· *Today, the day ahead*—You feel confident about your achievements because you know they are a result of your commitment and hard work, rather than just luck. You are not afraid of losing them because you can rebuild them with ease.

· *Today, in love*—This is a time of intense passion and attraction in your relationship, where your sex appeal is drawing interest from those around you. If you're single, it's a great time to flirt and take the first step toward someone who has caught your eye.

· *Today, at work*—You have performed exceptionally well at work, showing perseverance and intelligence in overcoming difficulties. As a result, you can expect to receive well-deserved recognition in the form of a promotion or pay raise, and you will earn the respect and esteem of your colleagues.

· *Self-reflection*—It's time to celebrate all the richness of life: have fun, unwind, and enjoy your hard-earned success. But be careful not to go overboard and fall into the traps of laziness and greed.

· *A symbol*—Today's symbol for reflection is the bench. Just as this seat stands firmly on its four legs, your achievements are built on a strong foundation of experience and wisdom.

SELF-ESTEEM

· *Today, the day ahead*— The challenges you faced to achieve your goals and finally grasp them, shining and solid, have highlighted your true abilities of intelligence, resilience, and self-sacrifice. By believing in yourself, you were able to reap the rewards of your hard work.

· *Today, in love*— If in the past you felt held back by shyness, thinking you weren't good enough or couldn't give enough, now you know your worth and what you want from your relationship, and you are content in a balanced situation. This newfound inner awareness is reflected in your ability to communicate with loyalty, clarity, and simplicity.

· *Today, at work*—You have always kept a low profile and worked hard with dedication and passion, giving your all to reach the company's goals. Today you will be publicly recognized for your achievements. Don't be modest—let your self-esteem be nourished by these well-deserved rewards.

· *Self-reflection*—Shyness and modesty are often lauded as virtues, but if taken to an extreme, they can obscure your self-perception, preventing you from recognizing your true abilities. Rediscover the ability to surprise yourself, remove the veil, and radiate your light without fear of slipping into arrogance; you are wise enough to prevent it.

· *A symbol*—Today, let the red cap be a symbol to reflect on. It symbolizes an active mind that is full of bold thinking, assertiveness, and passion. These are all gifts that you possess and have used to achieve success. Attitude is key: if you are open to receiving, the universe will give you all that you desire and more.

Happiness · Family

The Ten of Cups symbolizes the end of an emotional journey. Usually, it signifies the attainment of joy, contentment, and bliss in relationships with others. Always remember that life is best enjoyed with the people you love.

Choose what kind of energy you want to draw from the Ten of Cups today:

Family, Joy, Love

FAMILY

· *Today, the day ahead*—True success comes from forming strong connections with those around you, sharing feelings and life events with your family, the place that holds your heart.

· *Today, in love*—You have reached a state of bliss where love and harmony are shared. Now is the time to pursue your dreams, whether it's marriage, strong friendships, reconciliations, or the realization of a desired pregnancy. Build a strong home where you can experience your most intimate emotions in peace and harmony.

· *Today, at work*—At work, creating a close-knit team with shared values and mutual support is key to creating a sense of "family" within the environment.

· *Self-reflection*— What does family mean to you? Society's views on this concept can vary greatly, but it's universally accepted that one of the world's biggest issues is the trend of individualization and the loneliness that follows. Family, then, is a place to go back to for that comforting embrace that helps you reconnect with yourself and your origins, in harmony with your spirit.

· *A symbol*—Reflecting on the symbol of the home today can bring a sense of stability and comfort. It can be a refuge from the hustle and bustle of everyday life, a place to reconnect with your inner self and to open your heart to those you care about most.

JOY

· *Today, the day ahead*—You have demonstrated commitment, resilience, and dedication, and as a result, you will receive abundant gifts, wishes, and blessings.

· *Today, in love*—The relationship you have always dreamed of will come knocking at your door, and with it, wedding bells will ring. All your desires and aspirations will be fulfilled, leading to complete emotional fulfillment. You will feel thrilled to make commitments that will pave the way for a joyous and harmonious future.

· *Today, at work*—Great news has arrived at work! Your talents are highly valued, and there's a good chance you may be up for a pay raise or promotion soon.

· *Self-reflection*—Your life is filled with harmony, and you are grateful for all the gifts you have received. You are free from conflict and the vibrant colors of freedom allow you to live the life of your dreams, filled with love and serenity. You radiate and are surrounded by this positive energy.

· *A symbol*—Today's symbol for reflection is the rainbow. You have completed a spiritual cycle, and now that the rainy days are behind you, life is shining in all its colors. This is a promise of blessings from heaven to seal your accomplishments.

LOVE

· *Today, the day ahead*—Today, you will experience a new sense of harmony as everything that once seemed in opposition or a cause of conflict now shows its complementary nature. This realization will dispel all fears and tensions, reaffirming the love you feel and bringing you a shining harmony of purpose.

· *Today, in love*—A new romantic and joyful relationship may be on the horizon, or a long-term relationship could experience even greater happiness. Both require commitment and love, which will allow you to fully enjoy the pleasures you share with your loved one.

· *Today, at work*—You will be presented with a project that will allow you to utilize your skills and passion. As you work on this project, you will earn the respect of your colleagues, and it will feel like you are not just working but creating something beautiful for the world.

· *Self-reflection*—Trust your instincts and pursue your passions. You feel happy and inspired, and you are in harmony with yourself and those around you. Show generosity to others and stay true to your values. Pursue what makes you happy, as an act of self-love that you deserve. Your happiness will spread to the people around you.

· *A symbol*—You can reflect on the symbol of the couple today, not just as a relationship between two people who become everything for each other, but also as the loving union of opposites in the soul. In both cases, you have everything you desire from life and will continue to do so.

PAGE of CUPS.

Creativity · Kindness

The Page of Cups is a highly imaginative, creative, and receptive person. They have a unique ability to listen with tact and sensitivity, and their energy resides in the heart rather than the head. The Page embodies qualities of gentleness, tolerance, and emotional intelligence, with a keen ability to feel and connect deeply with others.

Choose what kind of energy you want to draw from the Page of Cups today:
Creativity, Sensitivity, Surprise

CREATIVITY

· *Today, the day ahead*—It's the perfect moment to bring a touch of imagination and a fresh perspective to your approach toward life and those around you. Embrace this urge to try something new and extraordinary, and let your creativity shine through various art forms. Don't hesitate to follow your inspiration.

· *Today, in love*—When it comes to love, past breakups, misunderstandings, and disappointments can often cause us to lose our sense of adventure and innocence. However, today presents an opportunity to reclaim that drive and creativity and reignite the spark that fueled your first love. Keep in mind that every day is a new chance for happiness, so embrace it as a beautiful challenge!

· *Today, at work*—Your creative vision, imagination, and intuition are really paying dividends! Follow your gut and you'll be rewarded with fresh and unforeseen job prospects and investment opportunities coming your way.

· *Self-reflection*—Reignite your inner child: young, liberated, creative, and inspired. Don't stifle your emotional and intuitive strength, let your creativity take flight and you will start the rebirth of your emotionally vibrant and productive self, allowing that sense of freedom to come back into your life.

· *A symbol*—Today, you can reflect on the symbol of the tunic with flowers as a representation of a new season of the soul. Let inner peace and the power of your passions come together to create a garden of creativity and inspiration. Now is the time to tap into your artistic abilities and rekindle the talents you have been neglecting.

SENSITIVITY

· *Today, the day ahead*—Trust your gut feeling and instincts—they're trying to tell you something! Your intuition is incredibly powerful, and you might be receiving messages from your subconscious mind through dreams or synchronistic encounters with significant individuals. Don't underestimate the significance of this subconscious channel simply because it can't be explained logically. It's important to listen to your inner voice right now.

· *Today, in love*—You're probably more likely to openly express your emotions now, so don't hesitate to let them show and reveal your sensitive side. Allow your heart to guide you in the right direction.

· *Today, at work*—Trust your gut feelings today; it's a great time to start a new project. Have the courage to dream big, and everything will become possible.

· *Self-reflection*—When it comes to your personal life, try to balance your emotional responses with reason. Don't let the intensity of your emotions cloud your judgment. Use that energy as fuel to help your new projects thrive.

· *A symbol*—Today's symbol for reflection is the sea. Emotions are like the sea's waters, with unfathomable depths. Even when the waves appear calm and serene, a sudden storm can arise at any moment. It's essential to familiarize yourself with that sea and gain a complete understanding of your own emotions. After all, only you can be the captain of your soul.

SURPRISE

· *Today, the day ahead*—Something delightfully unexpected may pop up in your life. Embrace it with open arms and welcome it with joy.

· *Today, in love*—You might unexpectedly encounter love today. This may manifest in various ways, perhaps with a pregnancy or through meeting someone who exhibits youthful exuberance and a zest for life. Such an experience has the potential to infuse your life with the purest of emotions, echoing the blissful moments of youth.

· *Today, at work*—A better job and new investment opportunities will unexpectedly come knocking at your door, bringing prosperity, good fortune, business success, and a possible salary increase.

· *Self-reflection*—Embracing and cherishing new experiences is like being inspired. They're like seeds that, if left uncared for, will simply wither away. But if we nurture them, they can bear fruit and bring forth exciting new opportunities.

· *A symbol*—Take a moment to think about the symbolism of the fish in the cup. It represents new beginnings, purity, and fertility—blessings that can take you by surprise and leave you feeling bewildered, since they come from unexpected contexts. Nonetheless, they speak to the heart and urge you to welcome them into your life. By being receptive to the unexpected, you can reap great rewards.

Devotion · Idealism

The Knight of Cups symbolizes someone who is on a journey
of personal development, but who still has more to learn. Their strength
lies in their ability to connect to their emotions and intuition,
which provide them with insight and direction.

Choose what kind of energy you want to draw from the Knight of Cups today:

Devotion, Idealism, Intelligence

DEVOTION

· *Today, the day ahead*—Try not to rush into action with your big plans and ideas. It's important to take your time and ensure that the timing is right, since rushing things can often result in less than ideal outcomes. Stay focused on the end goal, and you'll be more likely to achieve it.

· *Today, in love*—Your intentions are noble, and it's clear that you're aware of your inner power that comes from the unity of energy between your heart and mind. However, don't let this strength become a way to dominate others. Instead, offer yourself as a source of support to help others along their life path.

· *Today, at work*—You don't need to rush or force yourself to achieve your goals. Instead, find a pace that you're comfortable with and stick with it until you reach your objective. It's crucial to strike a balance between your ideas and actions, making sure that you're taking active steps to reach your goals and fulfill your ambitions.

· *Self-reflection*—Take this time in your life to explore your passions and big ideas. Your heart and mind are aligned, so allow yourself to pursue new goals with dedication and the willingness to make sacrifices.

· *A symbol*—Take a moment to contemplate the symbolism of the white horse. This image embodies a bright and noble life force that serves as a faithful companion to the person it accompanies. This reflects the essence of your highest mind.

IDEALISM

· *Today, the day ahead*—Your life values form the bedrock of your nature and have matured over time through your experiences. When making decisions, you tend to rely on these values that are deeply ingrained in your heart rather than logic alone. You are guided by human warmth, friendship, and love, and tend to make choices that align with those values without much deliberation.

· *Today, in love*—You seem to have a romantic view of love, but don't be too rigid in your expectations. Even with its imperfections, love can still be beautiful and genuine. In fact, those imperfections can often be the key to a successful relationship.

· *Today, at work*—You tend to stick to your professional ethics at work, which can be a good thing when compromising them would go against your values. However, if you're offered a different work project than what you had planned, and it doesn't conflict with your moral values, it's best to remain flexible and open-minded instead of becoming entrenched in your current position.

· *Self-reflection*—If you're embarking on a new creative project, focus on turning your imaginative ideas into tangible results. For your ideals to truly come to life and take on shape outside of the realm of fantasy, they require practical actions. Try not to get too caught up in a romanticized view of life and instead focus on concrete steps to bring your vision into reality.

· *A symbol*—Reflect on the symbol of the tunic decorated with fish. It represents the connection between your consciousness and creativity. The two combine to fuel your passions and emotional connections with others. Take some time to explore your emotional sphere without getting overwhelmed by it.

INTELLIGENCE

· *Today, the day ahead*—Your mind is active and constantly churning with ideas. You possess a vivid imagination and creativity, and you balance it with a healthy dose of rationality to ensure that your intellectual liveliness translates into thoughtful and wise actions that help you overcome obstacles in life.

· *Today, in love*—Take the time to explore your options, focus on personal growth, and don't be afraid to take the first step by being proactive and taking initiative.

· *Today, at work*—You may have to make some decisions that can potentially change your work routine, leading to better job opportunities in the long run. To achieve these rewards, you must take the necessary steps and step outside your comfort zone.

· *Self-reflection*—You are feeling motivated and decisive, and your actions are aligned with your thoughts. You possess the ability to consider the consequences of your decisions carefully and wisely. Do not hesitate to move forward confidently and steadily, as this is the key to success in all your endeavors.

· *A symbol*—You can reflect today on the symbols of the winged helmet and boots. You possess a sharp intellect and can thoroughly evaluate the various aspects of a decision before taking action. This is a valuable skill and a gift that sets you apart. Your ideas have the potential to soar above the rest, but it's essential that you can also put them into action. Otherwise, they'll remain just as mere mental exercises, which would be a great loss.

Affection · Empathy

The Queen of Cups is often associated with love, empathy,
and compassion. This card is overflowing with sensitivity and emotion.
She is like a lover, friend, or mother who speaks to you with both tenderness
and objectivity, providing you with the guidance and advice you need,
especially during challenging times.

Choose what kind of energy you want to draw from the Queen of Cups today:
Maturity, Empathy, Motherhood

MATURITY

· *Today, the day ahead*—You recognize the significance of the sacrifices, changes, and risks you are willing to take. You accept both the honors and responsibilities that come with it, without feeling overly proud or overwhelmed. You strive to maintain a balance between your ideals and the reality, so that you can maintain your unique identity.

· *Today, in love*—Everything is going well in your relationship right now. Maintaining harmony, understanding, and communication are key to continuing to make progress. Singles are now emotionally ready to start a new relationship.

· *Today, at work*—You will offer and receive impartial and thoughtful advice. Now is not the time to be self-centered, but to help your new hires or struggling coworkers by sharing the expertise you have acquired.

· *Self-reflection*—The purpose of life is to nurture the soul, rather than accumulating material possessions or achieving social status. These are ephemeral pleasures that can never bring contentment to a soul that has not realized its full potential.

· *A symbol*—Today's symbol for reflection is the crown, which represents an enlightened individual who has integrated their emotions and thoughts and has attained a wisdom that cannot be diminished by time or negative events. This person has achieved a connection between heaven and earth, allowing their mind to serve as a vehicle for understanding the world around them.

EMPATHY

· *Today, the day ahead*—You have a natural ability to connect with your emotions, which has led you to develop a strong sense of empathy. This enables you to help those around you make sense of their emotions in a compassionate and sensitive manner.

· *Today, in love*—You are a source of comfort and security for your loved ones. Your genuine care and understanding, combined with your emotional stability and consistency, make you a safe haven for those in need of emotional support. However, it is important to remember to take care of yourself and not become overwhelmed.

· *Today, at work*—Your capacity for understanding and connecting with others has not only been beneficial in gaining clients, but also in fostering a work environment of collaboration and friendship. If you keep this up, you could be in line for a promotion or a major career shift.

· *Self-reflection*—You have an extraordinary ability to understand and relate to other people's perspectives, which has led you to become deeply interested in others. You have honed your listening skills, even when it comes to your own emotions, and you are able to interpret them with a gentle and compassionate attitude. You don't like to create walls between yourself and others, but sometimes it is necessary.

· *A symbol*—Today's meditation symbol is the silver robe. It's like a mirror that reflects the innermost secrets of others, allowing them to glimpse their own mysteries. In the same way, your soul can reflect the souls of those you meet and understand them empathically.

MOTHERHOOD

· *Today, the day ahead*—Your presence is comforting and inviting; you connect with the world and to others through the expressions of love and kindness you share so generously.

· *Today, in love*—You have the natural ability to be an amazing parent—a tenderness, protectiveness, sensitivity, and guidance that you feel for all living beings. This instinct also makes you a loving and devoted partner.

· *Today, at work*—Trust your advisors and build strong relationships with them, especially if they are mature women; approach them with an open heart, forgive and let go of any resentment. Doing this will ensure your efforts are successful and will lead to a significant increase in your income and profits.

· *Self-reflection*—The warmth of motherly love that resides in your heart is both gentle and powerful. It is a strength that could help to save the world, even if it's just the world around you. Showing poise, balance, and civility are examples of how you can do this. You don't need to be a hero, just be your authentic self.

· *A symbol*—Today, you can reflect on the symbols of fish, shells, and water lilies, which allude to the birth of Venus, the goddess of fertility, beauty, and love. Everything within you is life, and everything you encounter radiates beauty and grace. Your emotions can be expressed with gentle assurance and trust.

Balance · Harmony

The King of Cups, seated upon his throne, rules over a tumultuous sea.
He is in full command of the emotions of the unconscious, allowing
them to be expressed openly while keeping them in check.

Choose what kind of energy you want to draw from the King of Cups today:
Harmony, Diplomacy, Charm

HARMONY

· *Today, the day ahead*—Find balance by allowing reason to merge with emotion, not letting it overpower or suppress it. At a fundamental level, both your conscious and unconscious selves yearn for fulfillment and the pursuit of your true potential.

· *Today, in love*—It is a truly magical moment when two souls vibrate in perfect harmony. It cannot be sought or forced; it is something that happens spontaneously as the result of a journey of growing closer and understanding each other. It is a precious treasure to be cherished and remembered.

· *Today, at work*—Finding the right balance within a diverse team is no easy feat, but when you do, it can be the key to achieving extraordinary results. Look for a leader who can confidently bring together the different perspectives and steer the team in the right direction without any doubt.

· *Self-reflection*—One of the ultimate objectives of a spiritual growth journey is to align your unconscious and conscious spheres. The King of Cups card represents that this is an achievable goal that requires the right mindset and the ability to navigate the ebbs and flows of your inner self without being overwhelmed by them.

· *A symbol*—The fish-shaped amulet worn by the King of Cups is a symbolic representation of the attainment of harmony between your conscious and unconscious spheres. It is not necessary to suppress your emotions, nor should you allow them to overpower you. Rather, you must learn to navigate through them, flowing with the current without being swept away.

DIPLOMACY

· *Today, the day ahead*—At times, it's essential to step in and mediate: when different demands and wishes clash, when opposing views don't match up, and when seemingly incompatible needs need to be reconciled. It may be necessary to bring in a third party to help resolve the situation.

· *Today, in love*—Truth is like the sun: it can bring warmth and be beneficial, but too much direct exposure can cause harm. Even in the most honest and genuine relationships, there is always a way to make communication more pleasant.

· *Today, at work*—When it's impossible to determine who is right and who is wrong, it's important to find someone impartial to mediate between the two sides. If you're in this situation, reach out to an outside source to help you come to a resolution. If you're asked to be the mediator, make sure to keep the perspectives of all parties in mind, and don't let your own feelings get in the way.

· *Self-reflection*—Sometimes you find yourself in a state of inner conflict, as different desires and needs clash within you. This can lead to a feeling of frustration that you can't even explain, as you choose to prioritize one desire over another. Finding a way to balance these competing needs within yourself is the key to eliminating this negative emotion.

· *A symbol*—The cup and scepter held by the King signify the capacity to discover a middle ground between conflicting interests, even in times of chaos. It is always possible to find balance.

CHARM

· *Today, the day ahead*—At times, appealing to reason or emotion alone is not enough; it takes the charisma of a leader to transcend both. Now is the time to set aside any doubts and hesitations, regardless of whether you are the one leading or someone else is.

· *Today, in love*— It's easy to confuse admiration for someone with love. Take a step back and try to understand where your feelings are coming from. If you're the one being admired, it's important to take on the responsibility that comes with being in the spotlight.

· *Today, at work*—While it is often beneficial to pose questions and inquiries about the path you should take, sometimes it is best to trust in the intuition and expertise of those in charge.

· *Self-reflection*—Simply by being your authentic self, you can be an inspiration to others.

· *A symbol*—The regal crown atop the King of Cups symbolizes a luminous charm, a balanced guide who can help you navigate stormy waters.

Prosperity · Beginning

The Ace of Pentacles typically signifies the initiation of a tangible project and is often considered a favorable card. It marks the inception of an undertaking, the establishment of a concrete reality that may not necessarily be linked to finances but is nevertheless grounded in materiality.

Choose what kind of energy you want to draw from the Ace of Pentacles today:

Prosperity, Beginning, Foundations

PROSPERITY

· *Today, the day ahead*—Something will make your day more fulfilling and meaningful. Be ready to embrace whatever the day has in store for you.

· *Today, in love*—It's a great time to commit to something that will help your relationship grow and thrive in the future. Invest in something concrete and enjoy the benefits of a more enriched relationship.

· *Today, at work*—Invest in yourself today and you'll reap bigger rewards tomorrow. Making a small sacrifice now can go a long way in helping you achieve your goals.

· *Self-reflection*—Take a moment to reflect on the abundance of resources, both tangible and intangible, that you have at your disposal. How can you make the best use of them for yourself and others? Don't waste any of these precious gifts.

· *A symbol*—Today's symbol to reflect on is lushly growing flowers. The abundance with which they flourish represents the material and immaterial wealth that this card expresses.

BEGINNING

· *Today, the day ahead*—It's the perfect day to start something new in any field that you enjoy. Starting something new can bring some apprehension, but don't let your fears hold you back. Take the plunge with confidence.

· *Today, in love*—A simple glance, a few exchanged words, or even a letter could ignite something new today. Whether it develops further or not is up to you.

· *Today, at work*—Do you have a new project in mind? What are you waiting for to get started? Today is also an excellent day to make a change to your daily routine.

· *Self-reflection*—This might be the ideal time to learn a new skill, enroll in a course, or pursue a new hobby.

· *A symbol*—The symbol to reflect on today is the arch in the hedge, which represents the doorway to a new journey. It's the starting point for something unprecedented.

FOUNDATIONS

· *Today, the day ahead*—Today is a time to reflect on the strength of your foundations. The stronger they are, the better equipped you will be to withstand any challenges that may arise.

· *Today, in love*—What makes a strong and loving relationship? Affection, understanding, attraction, trust, and many other factors. If the foundation of your relationship is solid, then it can withstand anything that may come your way.

· *Today, at work*—No matter what your job is, sometimes it's important to go back to basics, to the foundation. Today may be the perfect day to do just that.

· *Self-reflection*—Your personality is complex and multifaceted, but what lies at the heart of your being? Is it love, ambition, the pursuit of happiness, or something else? It's important to remind yourself of your core motivation from time to time.

· *A symbol*—Today, the symbol to reflect on is the hand ready to bestow, which represents a willingness to invest in the groundwork of a business. It serves as a reminder of the importance of establishing a strong foundation for future growth and success.

Change · Precariousness

The Two of Pentacles is here to prepare you for the ups and downs of life and encourage you to face them with balance and stability.

Choose what kind of energy you want to draw from the Two of Pentacles today:

Fluctuating Fortunes, Change, (Precarious) Balance

FLUCTUATING FORTUNES

· *Today, the day ahead*—Life is full of ups and downs, and it can be challenging to maintain balance. The trick is to approach everything with a sense of lightness and joy, as if you are dancing.

· *Today, in love*—All relationships have their ups and downs, and both are a natural part of the journey of lasting love. By staying committed and persistent, you can navigate through the difficult times and look forward to the happy moments that will come again.

· *Today, at work*—Every job comes with its ups and downs. Try not to get too carried away during the good times or too discouraged during the bad times.

· *Self-reflection*—Mood swings can be likened to the ebb and flow of the tides, and it's crucial to be mindful of them and strive to maintain a sense of equilibrium.

· *A symbol*—Today, the symbol to focus on is the juggler's hands, which remind us of the constant ups and downs in life and the importance of finding balance.

CHANGE

·*Today, the day ahead*—Things are always changing, and you need to be prepared for whatever comes your way. Don't be caught off guard when change inevitably arrives.

· *Today, in love*—Love is an ever-evolving entity that needs to stay true to itself. Introducing something new into a relationship helps to keep it vibrant and alive. Without any changes, the flame can fade, and emotions may die down.

· *Today, at work*—A change is on its way, whether it's welcomed or not, even if it's only in the form of a shift in your routine or habits. The key to reaping its benefits is to gracefully welcome it.

· *Self-reflection*—Change is both difficult and inevitable. We undergo transformations every day, yet we remain true to ourselves. You can't prevent change from occurring, and trying to control it can be complicated. It's better to embrace it and gently guide yourself toward the desired evolution, accepting the changes that come along the way.

· *A symbol*—The infinity ribbon being juggled represents the countless opportunities that the universe has in store for you, all within your reach.

(PRECARIOUS) BALANCE

· *Today, the day ahead*—You may find it challenging to balance the different demands of your life. It's important to make time and space for everything and everyone, even if it means not being able to fully devote yourself to any one thing or person.

· *Today, in love*—Finding a balance between your own needs and those of your partner is never an easy task. However, by communicating your difficulties and trusting in your partner's understanding, you can do your best to achieve a healthy balance in the relationship. Remember that both of you are called upon to do the same.

· *Today, at work*—Strive to do your best by openly communicating your challenges and relying on the support and understanding of your colleagues and superiors. Achieving a sense of balance can improve your performance in all areas of your life.

· *Self-reflection*—Each person has their own unique formula for achieving balance, much like the organs in our bodies that help us maintain balance. While it may take some practice, we are all capable of finding this balance, including you.

· *A symbol*—The symbol for today is the juggler's feet, representing the delicate balance required to juggle multiple tasks. The key to achieving this balance is to approach it with a lightness and ease.

Skills · Collaboration

The Three of Pentacles portrays a skilled stonemason hard at work, showcasing his expertise and professionalism. This card highlights the value of a job well done, demonstrating the importance of respecting someone's skills and abilities in action.

Choose what kind of energy you want to draw from the Three of Pentacles today:
Planning, Collaboration, Skills

PLANNING

· *Today, the day ahead*—Having a clear plan of action is key to accomplishing something positive, especially today. Take the time to plan out the necessary steps, no matter how big or small, that will guide you toward your goal.

· *Today, in love*—Love also requires planning and projection into the future. Assess where your relationship currently stands and where it's headed. Do you need clarity on certain aspects, or can you envision the next steps clearly?

· *Today, at work*—Now that you have the necessary tools and knowledge, it's time to create a well-thought-out plan before you start working!

· *Self-reflection*—The most important project in your life revolves around yourself. Consider the kind of person you aspire to become, the direction you wish to take your existence, and how you can grow into your true self.

· *A symbol*—Take some time today to reflect on the arches that support the three pentacles. This symbol serves as a powerful reminder that without proper preparation, it is impossible to create works of lasting excellence.

COLLABORATION

· *Today, the day ahead*—Working together toward a common goal is not only beneficial, it is also often essential. Can you offer your assistance without being asked? Can you graciously accept the help that is offered to you?

· *Today, in love*—It's easy to forget, but relationships are a team effort. If there is no balance of effort and purpose, love is doomed to fail. Support, sacrifice, and backing can't be one-sided—an arch needs two pillars to stand.

· *Today, at work*—The importance of having a close-knit team for support cannot be overstated. When working together as a team, individual strengths are highlighted, and collaboration is made easier without any hesitation or delay.

· *Self-reflection*—While it's true that nobody knows you better than yourself, sometimes getting suggestions from others or considering a different perspective can be incredibly enlightening. It's important to remember that other people's opinions don't define you but gaining insight into how others see you can help you gain a better understanding of yourself.

· *A symbol*—As you reflect on today's symbol, the small circle that connects the three pentacles, it becomes evident that true success in life can only be achieved when we work together in harmony.

SKILLS

· *Today, the day ahead*—Knowledge is not just an end in itself; it can be a valuable guide in your daily life. Therefore, any kind of expertise should be respected, cultivated, and, if possible, shared.

· *Today, in love*—There's nothing wrong with seeking advice from friends or significant others to gain an external perspective and find fresh solutions for dealing with difficulties or doubts about yourself.

· *Today, at work*—If you're struggling with difficulties, seeking advice from someone with more experience can be helpful in coming to terms with them. It's perfectly normal to not know how to do everything and learning to identify the right person to turn to for guidance is an important skill to develop.

· *Self-reflection*—If you're looking to gain insight into yourself, seeking external help can be beneficial. While a psychologist is often the best option, there may be certain circumstances where tools like Tarot can still help.

· *A symbol*—Take a moment to reflect on the looks exchanged between the stonemason, the merchant, and the monk. These looks reveal a mutual respect for each other's skills, as well as a willingness to listen and trust one another.

FOUR OF PENTACLES

Solidity · Parsimony

The Four of Pentacles signifies stability, wealth, and immobility. It's a powerful reminder of how challenging it can be to let go of certainties and take risks, and how easily attachment to things can transform into entrenchment.

Choose what kind of energy you want to draw from the Four of Pentacles today:
Solidity, Parsimony, Power

SOLIDITY

· *Today, the day ahead*—You have the necessary resources to tackle any challenges that may come your way today. The question is, how much are you willing to risk?

· *Today, in love*—The idea of "two hearts and a home" may sound romantic, but it's important to consider practical aspects before taking the next step in your relationship. Make sure your foundation is strong before taking a leap of faith.

· *Today, at work*—Sometimes taking the safe route may be the best choice when considering a new job opportunity. However, if you're starting something new, you can rely on the strength of your foundation.

· *Self-reflection*—It's natural to have some level of certainty in life but having too much of it can hinder personal growth and maturation. On the other hand, having no certainties can leave you feeling lost and lacking direction. Finding a balance between the two is challenging but crucial for personal development.

· *A symbol*—The two pentacles at the feet of the figure in the Arcanum remind you of the importance of having a solid foundation to support you, while also warning not to become too attached to your sources of income, whether material or immaterial.

PARSIMONY

· *Today, the day ahead*—It's perhaps not the best time to invest emotional energy or resources. It can be wise to keep a reserve for difficult times that may arise.

· *Today, in love*—You may feel tempted to rush into things in your romantic life. The Four of Pentacles suggests taking time to reflect, slowing things down if necessary, and not abandoning your principles just for the sake of adventure or novelty.

· *Today, at work*—It's a good idea to slow down and take time to think things through.

· *Self-reflection*—Just as you would in a long journey, it's important to pace yourself and conserve your energy to reach your destination safely and steadily. The same principle applies when embarking on the journey of self-discovery.

· *A symbol*—The symbol of the money shielded by the man tightly wrapping his arms around it represents the importance of protecting what is most valuable to you and not exposing it to unnecessary risks.

· *Today, the day ahead*—The way power is exercised can determine whether it is used as a means of authority or oppression.

· *Today, in love*—When it comes to relationships today, consider whether the power is balanced or not. If there is an imbalance, how is the power being used by those in control? These are important points to question.

· *Today, at work*—It's crucial to give proper thought to how you treat your subordinates. Are you treating them fairly or just relying on your position of power? If you have a superior, it's important to consider how you handle the pressure and demands from them.

· *Self-reflection*—It's important to remember that you hold the ultimate power over yourself. Though it may be alluring to convince yourself that change is impossible, it is merely a beguiling deception that does not hold true.

· *A symbol*—The man depicted wears a crown, symbolizing power, prestige, and wealth. Yet it's crucial to keep in mind that power can also be a great burden to bear.

FIVE OF PENTACLES

Destitution · Refuge

The Five of Pentacles shows two impoverished individuals, visibly distressed. Nevertheless, a ray of hope filters through the stained glass, providing some solace. This card signifies that you may encounter challenging periods along your journey and emphasizes the need for patience and perseverance.

Choose what kind of energy you want to draw from the Five of Pentacles today:
Destitution, Illness, Refuge

DESTITUTION

· *Today, the day ahead*—You may be currently experiencing a difficult time, or one may be looming soon. Whether it be material or immaterial hardships, they present challenges that can serve as an opportunity to prioritize what truly matters in your life.

· *Today, in love*—Limited finances can be a challenging obstacle for even the closest of couples to overcome. The encouraging news is that no economic condition is too inconvenient for a couple that remains united and committed, even amid difficulties. While it's important not to let a temporary lack of money ruin a genuine love, if someone is pulling away solely due to financial reasons, it provides an opportunity to reevaluate the true value of their feelings.

· *Today, at work*—It's becoming more and more common to encounter challenging times at work, such as job loss or difficulty finding employment. The Five of Pentacles encourages perseverance, reminding you that although the road ahead may be arduous and lengthy, there is still hope for finding solace and comfort.

· *Self-reflection*—How do you typically respond to challenges? Are you able to navigate the difficult moments that life presents, or will present, to you? Do you possess the fortitude to overcome these obstacles and set yourself on a path toward a brighter future?

· *A symbol*—The ragged clothes worn by the beggars in the card symbolize their poverty. Yet their posture is dignified, serving as a reminder that no situation of destitution can deprive you of your inherent dignity.

ILLNESS

· *Today, the day ahead*—We all experience periods of ill health throughout our lives, some of which may be temporary. But each time we can overcome it, we come out a little stronger.

· *Today, in love*—Romantic relationships can often manifest in unhealthy ways, such as material or psychological dependency, excessive control, manipulation, or even a desire to inflict harm on one's partner. Being able to identify these signs early on can help prevent them from becoming more serious and recurring issues.

· *Today, at work*—The workspace and environment you work in can have a big impact on your well-being and health. Have you taken the time to assess how respectful it is of your health and safety? It may be worth assessing thoroughly.

· *Self-reflection*—If you feel a general uneasiness, a need to take a break, or chronic fatigue, don't ignore these signs. Your body and mind need regular rest to stay healthy and avoid getting sick.

· *A symbol*—Take a moment to reflect on the symbol of the crutches held by the person on the left. Assess what kind of support system your own challenging health issues may need.

REFUGE

· *Today, the day ahead*—The illuminated stained glass window serves as a reminder that even in the most challenging situations, there is always a glimmer of hope and the promise of a safe, bright, and warm haven.

· *Today, in love*—When life throws unexpected challenges at you and your partner, it's crucial to be there for each other and provide comfort and support.

· *Today, at work*—Staying within your comfort zone can be necessary at times and not always a bad thing in the workplace.

· *Self-reflection*—There are special memories that hold a special place within each of us, representing bright moments of comfort, protection, and love. These memories serve as a soothing reminder of those times when we felt truly safe and comforted. It is important to know how to access and rediscover these memories, as they can provide you with a source of comfort and peace whenever you need it.

· *A symbol*—The illuminated stained glass window serves as a symbol for your reflection. It represents the idea that sometimes even the smallest glimmer of hope, like the light shining through stained glass, can help us endure the most challenging of times. Have you ever considered that you could be that same source of light for others? In times of darkness, being a beacon of hope and inspiration for those around you can make all the difference.

Sharing · Gratitude

The Six of Pentacles shows a wealthy merchant distributing donations generously to a pair of mendicants, indicating that with wealth comes great responsibility to give back. The card highlights the importance of generosity and the duty to share out at least a part of your wealth.

Choose what kind of energy you want to draw from the Six of Pentacles today:

Sharing, Gratitude, Equity

SHARING

· *Today, the day ahead*—It's commonly said that giving is more satisfying than receiving, and that holds true today.

· *Today, in love*—Love should be marked by the highest form of generosity—that's what the definition implies. It's all about giving what's most precious to you, which is yourself. So, do you embody this ideal? It's easy to give material objects, but can you give something far more valuable like your time, attention, and listening skills?

· *Today, at work*—Today would be a good day to help a colleague in need, even if it slows down your work temporarily. Your act of kindness will pay off in the long run.

· *Self-reflection*—St. Francis of Assisi once said, "It is in giving that we receive; in forgetting about ourselves that we find ourselves." These words serve as a gentle reminder that dedicating some of your time to helping others can bring you joy and fulfillment, even if you don't realize it. Sharing with your fellow human beings can be a rewarding experience.

· *A symbol*—The generous merchant's open hands and his serene appearance are a testament to the immense joy that comes from sharing what we have with those who are less fortunate.

GRATITUDE

· *Today, the day ahead*—The list of things to be grateful for each day is extensive; it's beneficial to begin by acknowledging the gifts you receive daily, not only from those who care for you, but from the universe itself.

· *Today, in love*—You cannot love merely out of appreciation, yet it is inconceivable to love someone without being thankful for their very being.

· *Today, at work*—It can be easy to be annoyed at work, but if you take the time to remember how demanding each job role is, you will be able to appreciate the sacrifices that everyone—subordinates, colleagues, and superiors—have to make.

· *Self-reflection*—Expressing a heartfelt thank you that comes from the depths of your being is not always simple. Yet, the feeling of liberation and satisfaction that follows is truly remarkable!

· *A symbol*—The mendicant's face is a powerful reminder of the importance of gratitude. It is a reminder that we should not take our blessings for granted, but instead express our appreciation for them. By showing your gratitude, you can be a source of joy and comfort to those around you, and in turn, be rewarded with a feeling of satisfaction. Gratitude is a two-way street, and the mendicant's face is a reminder of that.

EQUITY

· *Today, the day ahead*—The universe has bestowed us with many gifts, and our planet has the potential to provide enough resources to ensure everyone can live a dignified and joyful life, if only we shared them fairly. If you do not learn to share, you will not find anyone willing to help you grow.

· *Today, in love*—In matters of love, it is not a good idea to keep track of who is giving and receiving more. But always remember that if one person gives more than the other, it can easily tip the balance.

· *Today, at work*—If you are lucky enough to be in a leadership role, make sure to treat your colleagues fairly. Regardless of your position, you should be able to recognize everyone's strengths and weaknesses.

· *Self-reflection*—Having difficulty being fair to yourself is something many people struggle with. You can swing between being too forgiving and too critical of yourself. To gain a more objective perspective, try to look at yourself from the outside. This can help you to assess your achievements and failures more accurately.

· *A symbol*—The merchant holds the balanced scales in his left hand, symbolizing the equitable distribution of goods, as well as the merits and demerits, that the Six of Pentacles represents.

SEVEN OF PENTACLES

Disappointment · Perseverance

The Seven of Pentacles depicts a man who has been carefully monitoring the results of his hard work. His expression of discontent implies that he hasn't quite achieved what he had set out to do; however, the flourishing plant indicates that his efforts have not been completely fruitless.

Choose what kind of energy you want to draw from the Seven of Pentacles today:

Disappointment, Discouragement, Frustration

DISAPPOINTMENT

· *Today, the day ahead*—It is possible that you don't get the results you hoped for, or that your hard work is not rewarded. However, you ought to consider how much of this outcome is realistic and how much of it is due to having unrealistic expectations.

· *Today, in love*—It's totally normal to feel unsatisfied with your partner from time to time. But before voicing your concerns, take a moment to reflect on whether your expectations were realistic in the first place.

· *Today, at work*—It's a well-known fact that feeling unfulfilled at work and not getting the recognition you deserve for your hard work are more the norm than the exception. There's no doubt that this frustration is often completely justified, so it's crucial to acknowledge that sulking and dwelling on the issue is not what is going to change the situation.

· *Self-reflection*—Do you really want to base your satisfaction with your efforts solely on the material rewards you receive? Wouldn't it be better to recognize that the greatest reward is knowing that you gave it your all?

· *A symbol*—The man's hunched shoulders, are a symbolic indication of his profound dissatisfaction with the results of his labor. This weight can poison the soul and leave you feeling immobile, needing the support of a stick. The Seven of Pentacles card offers an invitation to let go of this disappointment and move forward.

DISCOURAGEMENT

· *Today, the day ahead*—Sometimes the weight of existence can feel overwhelming, making it seem impossible to regain confidence in the future.

· *Today, in love*—Sometimes things simply don't work out, even if both parties have given their all. It may not be necessary to end the relationship entirely, but it is crucial to identify and address the aspects that are causing problems.

· *Today, at work*—You might have taken a big risk. It's wise to take note of it and prepare for any possible consequences.

· *Self-reflection*—Finding the motivation to pick yourself up after a failure or disappointment can be tough, but it's essential. No one lives a life of constant success and contentment, so having the resilience to fight back is the key to transforming your future.

· *A symbol*—The man's disheartened look symbolizes discouragement. Nevertheless, it is precisely during this moment of introspection, reflecting on your failures, that you can gather the strength to rise again and continue on.

FRUSTRATION

· *Today, the day ahead*—Especially when you know you've done your best, not receiving the appropriate reward for your efforts can put you in a negative mindset that hovers between victimhood and apathy.

· *Today, in love*—There are some things that are just not worth trying to change, no matter how much effort you put into it. Instead of procrastinating and setting yourself up for disappointment, it's important to determine whether you can accept the situation as it is or if you need to redirect your efforts elsewhere.

· *Today, at work*—Sources of frustration appear to be numerous and almost never-ending. If you find yourself stuck in a vicious cycle, it's time to break free. Decisive action and a change of environment are necessary.

· *Self-reflection*—The road to spiritual maturity is filled with obstacles, consisting of moments of growth and stagnation—the latter often more frequent. It's important not to give in to frustration. Recognize that you're working within the framework of an evolutionary path.

· *A symbol*—The few fruits on the ground are likely the cause and certainly the symbol of human frustration, as they are left to rot in place. This serves as a reminder of the importance of eliminating the sources of our dissatisfaction, as constantly being reminded of them can only worsen the situation.

Precision · Perseverance

The Eight of Pentacles card shows a skilled craftsman at work, carrying out his work calmly and serenely. The card reminds you of the importance of being persistent and methodical, of applying yourself constantly to improve your skills.

Choose what kind of energy you want to draw from the Eight of Pentacles today:

Perseverance, Accuracy, Achievement

PERSEVERANCE

· *Today, the day ahead*—Approaching your goals with a determined and systematic approach is an effective way to avoid distractions and stay on track.

· *Today, in love*—When it comes to love, grand displays of passion, dramatic proclamations, and flashy gestures may seem impressive, but it's the everyday commitment, time, and effort invested in a relationship that ultimately make a difference.

· *Today, at work*—There's no need to search for extravagant solutions. Applying what you already know, and pushing through boredom, fatigue, and discouragement will lead you to the desired results.

· *Self-reflection*—Making a commitment is easy. Following through with it every day, without faltering in your resolutions, is much more challenging.

· *A symbol*—The continuous raising and lowering of the hammer symbolizes perseverance in the task at hand, whether it's one you've been assigned or one you've given yourself.

ACCURACY

· *Today, the day ahead*—Paying attention to detail can be the difference between a successfully completed work and one that falls short.

· *Today, in love*—Paying attention to the small details, unspoken signals, and nuances in your partner's language or behavior can be incredibly valuable in building a stronger connection, understanding what's wrong, and getting to know your partner better.

· *Today, at work*—It may be worthwhile to slow down and pay close attention to every little detail in your work. This will help you achieve better results or at the very least avoid making careless mistakes.

· *Self-reflection*—Today might be a great opportunity to focus on decluttering and organizing, both internally and externally. Take the time needed to make sure everything is in the right place.

· *A symbol*—The tip of the chisel symbolizes the importance of care and attention in all things. By paying attention to small details, you'll gain a better understanding of the big picture and be able to grasp every nuance. This approach is akin to the way a skilled artisan uses a chisel to create intricate carvings.

ACHIEVEMENT

· *Today, the day ahead*—The craftsman in the Eight of Pentacles not only has worked through the first parts of his task but has already achieved three-quarters of it! His hard work has been rewarded and the finish line is in sight.

· *Today, in love*—You may be close to achieving your goal, but you still need to put in some effort. Don't give up now—stay motivated to see the situation through.

· *Today, at work*—The first signs of success are beginning to show, and it's important to remain steady and finish what you have started.

· *Self-reflection*—Seeing the results of your hard work is always rewarding. Keep going and don't give up, even when faced with the most challenging parts of your journey.

· *A symbol*—Take a moment to reflect on the milestones you have surpassed and the accomplishments you have achieved in your life. The pentacles on the tree on the right are a tangible symbol of the hard work and success you have already achieved. Let the sense of pride in your accomplishments motivate and inspire you to continue your path with renewed energy.

Abundance · Legacy

The Nine of Pentacles depicts a woman in a vineyard, surrounded by lush, ripe grapes and coins. It symbolizes the abundance of material possessions that can be enjoyed in a peaceful and detached manner.

Choose what kind of energy you want to draw from the Nine of Pentacles today:

Abundance, Legacy, Self-Control

ABUNDANCE

· *Today, the day ahead*—The Nine of Pentacles brings an abundance of harvest, leading to a sense of physical and spiritual well-being, a complete satisfaction of needs, and the peace of mind that comes from having no financial worries.

· *Today, in love*—A deep love brings with it a profound sense of serenity, knowing that your relationship has the strength to overcome any challenge.

· *Today, at work*—Having the freedom to choose what tasks you want to work on each day is an incredible privilege. Not everyone is fortunate enough to have this kind of job, but we can all strive to find a job that we enjoy and that allows us to do the work we want to do.

· *Self-reflection*—Happy moments are truly invaluable, creating beautiful memories that will last a lifetime. A person with a wealth of positive memories will never experience the worst kind of poverty—poverty of the soul.

· *A symbol*—The grapes and the pentacles symbolize a plentiful harvest of the soul, self-assurance, and access to resources.

LEGACY

· *Today, the day ahead*—The wealth represented by the Nine of Pentacles doesn't have to be the result of your hard work—it could be an inheritance or something that has been passed down to you.

· *Today, in love*—Reflecting on the love that has been passed down through generations is one of the greatest gifts we can receive. Take some time to think about the values and lessons your parents and ancestors have shared with you. If you have or plan to have children, consider what kind of legacy you would like to leave them.

· *Today, at work*—Tradition plays an important role in even the most creative and innovative jobs, and it's something you can't ignore, even if you decide to go against it. But the knowledge of those who have gone before you is an invaluable resource; by learning from their mistakes, you can avoid making the same ones.

· *Self-reflection*—Your real legacy is the spiritual one, and each day you should strive to leave a better and improved version of yourself than the day before.

· *A symbol*—What proportion of your wealth is the result of your own hard work and dedication, and how much of it is due to the kindness and generosity of your ancestors? That's what the house behind the figure symbolizes—the legacy you have inherited.

SELF-CONTROL

· *Today, the day ahead*—If you learn to control your emotions, no one will be able to have power over you anymore. You are the one who gives others—and sometimes even things—power over yourself.

· *Today, in love*—Reckless reactions can take you and your relationship down a dangerous path. It's important to stay in control; when you're afraid, it can be easy to see things as more threatening than they really are. Taking a more relaxed approach to situations can help you see them for what they really are—usually not as bad as you think.

· *Today, at work*—It can be tempting to respond sharply to a superior or colleague, or to give a harsh reprimand to a subordinate, but this will only poison the atmosphere around you.

· *Self-reflection*—Emotionality can be a difficult companion to have, and it can stay with you for a long time. Learning to live with your emotions and finding harmony your mind, body, and spirit can help you find serenity.

· *A symbol*—The hawk perched calmly on the lady's arm is the ultimate symbol of self-control. It's no coincidence that it appears in the Nine of Pentacles, as a reminder that all the material and spiritual richness in this world can be lost in the blink of an eye if you don't maintain emotional control.

Family · Rest

The Ten of Pentacles shows a prosperous family patriarch surrounded
by loved ones, bringing him a profound sense of contentment and peace.
This card signifies the successful fulfillment of both career and relationship
aspirations, making it a highly auspicious and rewarding symbol.

Choose what kind of energy you want to draw from the Ten of Pentacles today:
Family, Legacy, Rest

FAMILY

· *Today, the day ahead*—Your efforts to build financial strength should serve the well-being of all your loved ones. If you've honed your talents, now is the time to reap the rewards through the love and gratitude of those close to you, as well as future generations.

· *Today, in love*—Love isn't solely about feeling good; it's about nourishing a family and cultivating relationships that bear fruit, benefiting all those involved and enriching their lives.

· *Today, at work*—If your job is consuming most of your time and energy, it's worth exploring ways to spend more time with loved ones. You might be pleasantly surprised at how refreshed and energized you feel, as well as how much more motivated and productive you become.

· *Self-reflection*—Remember that we are not solitary creatures—our relationships with others define us. No matter how much self-work you do, it's only meaningful if it improves your interactions with others.

· *A symbol*—The image of the young couple and child playing with dogs is a representation of the family unit that this symbol embodies. Throughout human history, the family—whether conventional or unconventional—has been a cornerstone of social life, and a vital component in achieving a sense of fulfillment.

LEGACY

· *Today, the day ahead*—Each of us will inevitably leave a mark on this world. So what kind of footprint do you want to leave behind?

· *Today, in love*—Leaving behind someone who will love you forever is the most lasting legacy.

· *Today, at work*—Do you feel comfortable passing on your knowledge and experience so that it won't be lost when you retire? Mentoring and guiding someone to carry on the path you have set is a rewarding and challenging responsibility, and it is important to find the right person to do so, who can take your knowledge and use it in their own way.

· *Self-reflection*—The greatest legacy you can leave behind for others is the testament of your own self and who you truly are.

· *A symbol*—The arch that begins above the patriarch's head and extends beyond the image serves as a symbol of how every achievement in life will carry forward into the future. While you may not live to see the full realization of your efforts, you will have played a role—for better or worse—in shaping the destiny of future generations.

REST

· *Today, the day ahead*—This card represents a well-deserved rest after working hard, surrounded by loved ones and enjoying the fruits of your labor. Whether you're already in this situation or aspire to be, this card serves as a reminder to take a moment to pause and appreciate the benefits of taking a break, whether it be a short respite or an extended period of rest.

· *Today, in love*—It's important to take a break from overthinking and simply enjoy the present moment, whether you're in a romantic relationship or not. Remember that you're not alone—you have a supportive network of friends and family who care about you and are ready to offer their support.

· *Today, at work*—It's essential to recharge your batteries occasionally. Taking time to relax and unplug is not only your right, it's also a great way to come back to your tasks feeling more energized and prepared. Today, make sure to take some time to unwind and recharge.

· *Self-reflection*—Take some time today to give yourself a break. Take a moment to relax and not feel any pressure. Take care of yourself in every way possible.

· *A symbol*—The image of the man, dressed in his finest, sitting and playing with his dogs in a peaceful and relaxed manner is a reminder of the importance of taking the time to appreciate the rewards of your hard work and savor them in a tranquil state.

Study · Progress

The Page of Pentacles strolls through a flowery meadow,
gazing at the golden coin in his hand, with a freshly plowed field
and a lush grove stretching out behind him. This card symbolizes the start
of a concrete venture or marking the beginning of a serene journey.

Choose what kind of energy you want to draw from the Page of Pentacles today:

Study, Perseverance, Progress

STUDY

· *Today, the day ahead*—The Page of Pentacles is a sign of a new and promising beginning, whether it be a journey of learning, the arrival of an apprentice, or a newfound interest in your life. It's an opportunity that requires your trust and faith.

· *Today, in love*—Taking it one step at a time is the best way to reach great goals. Keeping a clear focus on what's important and being methodical in your approach will help you get there. Starting your journey with enthusiasm and a plan of action is key to success.

· *Today, at work*—Today could be the perfect day to start learning something new, even if it's something completely different from what you're used to. After all, you never stop learning!

· *Self-reflection*—You can only become what you desire once you truly understand yourself.

· *A symbol*—The hat that frames the young man's face serves as a reminder of his unwavering focus on his studies. Let nothing distract you from your goals.

PERSEVERANCE

· *Today, the day ahead*—The Page of Pentacles knows that the best way to go far is to take it one step at a time. His aspirations are high, but he understands that success is not achieved through grand leaps but through hard work and dedication.

· *Today, in love*—Nurturing love requires daily attention to small gestures and kind words. While we all have the ability to be the perfect partner for a day, the real question is whether we can be a good partner for a lifetime.

· *Today, at work*—Maybe you've been working hard for months, maybe even years. You have no way of knowing whether you are close to achieving your goal or not, so don't give up now!

· *Self-reflection*—Perseverance and never giving up are the key ingredients to success. Taking small steps every day will eventually lead to big changes. It's not a secret, it's simply the only way to make progress.

· *A symbol*—Wildflowers symbolize the resilience of nature and life, surviving and thriving in all conditions and never giving up.

PROGRESS

· *Today, the day ahead*—Start your journey with confidence but also with a realistic outlook. Every giant was once a child, and every great accomplishment began with a single step. Take the first step toward a new project, a different path, and a new evolution.

· *Today, in love*—Starting a new relationship or a new chapter in your life is a delicate yet magical moment. The Page of Pentacles urges you to move forward with a mix of cautiousness and optimism, knowing that the journey ahead holds many rewards.

· *Today, at work*—The Page of Pentacles is encouraging you to venture into entrepreneurship, a decision that holds the potential for immense prosperity and triumph. Embrace this new direction and made your dreams come true.

· *Self-reflection*—No matter how far along you are on your journey of maturation, it's always important to remember to keep the enthusiasm of the first day alive. That way, you can ensure that your growth never ceases.

· *A symbol*—The meticulously sown field embodies the promise of a fruitful outcome.

Reliability · Stubbornness

The Knight of Pentacles is resolute in his pursuit of his objective,
firmly seated in his saddle and holding a coin carefully in his hand. His gaze
is pensive and wary, acknowledging that there is still a lengthy journey ahead,
but the end goal is gradually becoming visible on the horizon.

Choose what kind of energy you want to draw from the Knight of Pentacles today:
Reliability, Stubbornness, Responsibility

RELIABILITY

· *Today, the day ahead*—The Knight of Pentacles emphasizes the importance of taking action rather than relying on words alone. He reminds you to stay focused on your goal and not to get distracted by unnecessary conversations.

· *Today, in love*—It's time to make practical and achievable decisions to ensure your partner feels secure and confident in your relationship. Establishing a strong foundation for the future requires you to put your plans into motion and work diligently with a clear and specific direction.

· *Today, at work*—If you need help today, turn to someone or something you trust. If you don't have anyone to turn to, remember that you always have your own strength and resilience to rely on.

· *Self-reflection*—Your own wisdom is the most trustworthy source of knowledge you can rely on. Allow it to be your guide and you will rarely lose your way, even when there are no obvious signs to follow.

· *A symbol*—The knight's armor and his solid stance embody the unwavering commitment to his promises and intentions. He may not be the most creative companion, but his perseverance will assist you in achieving your desired outcome.

STUBBORNNESS

· *Today, the day ahead*—The Knight of Pentacles is unwavering in his pursuit of his goal, refusing to stray from his chosen path. However, this determined approach may leave him vulnerable to unforeseen challenges that could arise.

· *Today, in love*—While you may have a clear direction in mind, it's important to ensure that the other person is on the same wavelength. No one likes to be forced down a path they're not fully convinced of.

· *Today, at work*—If you're sure you're in the right, it's important to stand your ground and persist in your chosen path. But be careful not to be too stubborn, as having strong convictions can quickly turn into obstinacy.

· *Self-reflection*—You have the resilience to weather the storms of adversity, but it's worth considering if it's time to take a moment to reflect and reassess the path you've embarked upon.

· *A symbol*—The horse's tight reins keep you on a single path, preventing distractions and unwanted detours. However, this can also leave you unprepared for any unforeseen circumstances you may come across.

RESPONSIBILITY

· *Today, the day ahead*—It's time to take ownership of your responsibilities—no one else can do it for you. This card is calling you to take control of your own actions and decisions.

· *Today, in love*—You need to own up to the choices you've made and those you're about to make. Don't wait for things to reach a breaking point; confront the outcomes of your decisions with determination and take full responsibility for them.

· *Today, at work*—Despite any distractions, unexpected events, or disruptions from superiors and colleagues, you are ultimately responsible for the outcome of your work. Recognizing this is the initial step in holding yourself accountable and comprehending that, ultimately, your success or failure is primarily on you.

· *Self-reflection*—How many easy excuses do you always find for your actions? "He provoked me," "It was too tempting to resist," "I was entitled to it," "Anyone else would have reacted the same way," and so on. It's time to take responsibility for your choices and start acting like an adult.

· *A symbol*—The lifted visor on the Knight's armor symbolizes his fearlessness in showing his face and being personally accountable for his decisions and the path he chooses to take.

Fertility · Tranquility

The Queen of Pentacles sits on a lavishly adorned throne, intricately decorated with symbols of prosperity, wellness, and sensual pleasure. Her surroundings are lush, exuding an air of harmony and completeness. This card invokes a sense of harmonious fulfillment.

Choose what kind of energy you want to draw from the Queen of Pentacles today:

Abundance, Fertility, Tranquility

ABUNDANCE

· *Today, the day ahead*—You are in a fortunate position, for everything you need for your well-being is within reach. The abundance of life is evident around you, urging you to live in the present moment with great intensity.

· *Today, in love*—The Queen of Pentacles is a representation of your desires coming to fruition, whether it's reaching the peak of a relationship or realizing that you can lead a complete, abundant, and satisfying life on your own.

· *Today, at work*—"Maximizing results with minimal effort" is the motto of today. There's no shame in being able to use your skills wisely so that you can get the most out of your time and energy.

· *Self-reflection*—This card speaks to you of your self-actualization, independence, and stability. It reminds you that you have an abundance of potential and resources within you that you can access at any time. May you always be reminded of this truth.

· *A symbol*—The ripe fruits of the earth represent the abundance this Queen wants to share with you. Take a moment to appreciate the gifts you've received, as they are much more plentiful and valuable than you may realize.

FERTILITY

· *Today, the day ahead*—Abundance alone is not enough; it must be used to create new opportunities, spark new ideas, and bring about new experiences. Take a moment to appreciate the level of success you have achieved and use it to bring energy and resources to the world, thus continuing the cycle of life.

· *Today, in love*—Now is an ideal time to contemplate embarking on a new journey, starting a new relationship, or taking a risk you haven't yet dared to take.

· *Today, at work*—Today you are overflowing with ideas, an unstoppable fountain of creativity. Let these ideas run wild; there is no project, no matter how ambitious, that can't be explored today.

· *Self-reflection*—Everything you have achieved in life has been to enable you to give of yourself to others. Every step, every improvement, every success is a necessary part of helping to bring about positive change in those around you.

· *A symbol*—The quintessential symbol of fertility on this card is the rabbit peeking out from the lower right corner. Its outstretched ears and paws signify the importance of looking around and assessing your surroundings before jumping headlong into creating something new.

TRANQUILITY

· *Today, the day ahead*—The Queen of Pentacles exudes tranquility, creating a calm and serene atmosphere. It's a safe haven where your material needs are met, and worries can be kept at bay, at least for a while.

· *Today, in love*—Deep, true love brings calm and reassurance, comfort, and healing. It doesn't cause anxiety, palpitations, or trembling. This doesn't mean that it is dull or unexciting, but rather that the harmony that comes from a deep connection has the power to soothe.

· *Today, at work*—Today, it's important to take a moment to calm down and reflect. Find a quiet space to recharge, allowing you to return to the daily work battle feeling more energized and focused.

· *Self-reflection*—Rather than looking to external factors for happiness, focus on nurturing inner peace. This will open your eyes to the endless opportunities that exist within and around you.

· *A symbol*—The carved angel on the throne is a symbol of protection and guardianship over your inner peace and serves as a reminder that those who genuinely care for you will safeguard your tranquility.

Wealth · Concreteness

The King of Pentacles sits majestically on a grand throne,
adorned with symbols of wealth and power. He looks powerful
and content, like a benevolent ruler of the land before him.

Choose what kind of energy you want to draw from the King of Pentacles today:

Wealth, Building, Concreteness

WEALTH

· *Today, the day ahead*—The King of Pentacles has accumulated vast material wealth through consistent diligence and astute decision-making. This prosperity will endure and make a lasting impact, and you are within reach of achieving the goals you have set out.

· *Today, in love*—It's important not to overlook the significance of having financial security. Of course, love is more important than material possessions, but it's easier to focus on the power of emotions when you don't have money worries.

· *Today, at work*—Consistent effort is the key to attaining the success you deserve. You'll find it easy to stay focused on your goal today, and you'll experience a sense of peace and purpose in your work.

· *Self-reflection*—You are a complex and multifaceted individual, capable of expressing a myriad of emotions that echo throughout the universe. The human soul is a treasure trove of potential, like a diamond in the rough—it is up to you to uncover its brilliance.

· *A symbol*—The King's robes are a beautiful sight, adorned with intricate designs that blend seamlessly with the vines and other plants of the kingdom. They are a symbol of wealth and prosperity, but also serve as a reminder that true wealth is found in a harmonious relationship with the material world around you.

BUILDING

· *Today, the day ahead*—Don't let your time on this earth pass without leaving a legacy, something that will testify to who you are. Ask yourself what you can build or are already creating that will stand the test of time.

· *Today, in love*—Now is an ideal time to lay the groundwork for a project, to find a secure place to call home, and to start planning for yourself and the generations to come with a solid foundation in place.

· *Today, at work*—Today, more than ever, there is a need for you to produce tangible and visible results from your work. You might spend the day contemplating the raw materials of your craft, much like assembling bricks, until you finally construct a solid foundation that represents your hard work.

· *Self-reflection*—Engaging in a hands-on, manual activity and creating something tangible could be the soothing balm that your soul seeks today.

· *A symbol*—The buildings associated with the King of Pentacles represent his hard work and legacy to society. They serve as a tangible reminder that material wealth should not be solely for transient pleasure, but rather a foundation for leaving a lasting impact on the world.

CONCRETENESS

· *Today, the day ahead*—It's best to avoid daydreaming and instead focus on the essential and practical tasks at hand, as that's when you'll be most productive today.

· *Today, in love*—Express your affection with a tangible gesture. Not only will it mean more than a thousand words, but it will create a lasting memory that you both can cherish.

· *Today, at work*—Today, it's best to focus on tangible results rather than getting caught up in the details. Aim to get something concrete out of your work by avoiding making empty promises, grandiose statements, or too much theorizing.

· *Self-reflection*—Set yourself a realistic and achievable goal for today. Don't waste the day daydreaming and contemplating.

· *A symbol*—The throne decorated with bulls symbolizes practicality and stability. It serves as a reminder to take care of your foundation and ensure it is solid.

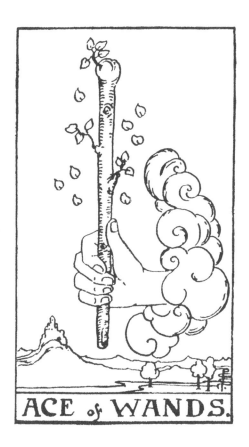

Strength · Self-Development

The Ace of Wands symbolizes the commitment to face life's challenges, the courage to take risks, and the determination to test your strength. It's a chance to feel alive and bring a new energy to everyday life.

Choose what kind of energy you want to draw from the Ace of Wands today:

Vitality, Opportunity, Diligence

VITALITY

· *Today, the day ahead*—Today is the perfect day to take the plunge and do something you've never had the confidence to try before. It could be an exhilarating experience that will motivate you to keep going; don't be afraid to take the risk!

· *Today, in love*—If you're in a relationship and want to rekindle the spark, why not plan something exciting together? It could be just the thing to reignite the flame. If you're single, keep your eyes peeled—you never know when a hot encounter might be on the horizon!

· *Today, at work*—Take advantage of the chances that come up this morning. They could be great for advancing your career. If you want to give your work a new boost, show enthusiasm and be ready to take risks.

· *Self-reflection*—Embrace every chance to grow and find fulfillment, whether it's a path, a hobby, or a journey. Today is the day to take the first step. Nurture enthusiasm for life and seize every opportunity!

· *A symbol*—Reflecting on the symbol of the mountain today can be a reminder of the goals we all strive to reach. It takes courage to take the first step and face the challenges of the journey, but it is the only way to reach the summit.

OPPORTUNITY

· *Today, the day ahead*—You will have the chance to embrace new and alluring challenges, presented to you with ease. It's up to you to assess whether it's worth taking a risk and committing to the end goal.

· *Today, in love*—If you were presented with the chance to go on an exciting journey today, what risks would you be willing to take? What emotions would you be ready to experience?

· *Today, at work*—Success in business requires two things: the determination to work hard and the courage to take risks. Every challenge involves a certain degree of risk, but it can be worth it if it leads to personal growth.

· *Self-reflection*—When feeling down and disconnected from those you love, it's important to reignite your inner fire and find hope in the journey ahead. There is always something to be passionate about and a new reason to keep going.

· *A symbol*—Reflecting on the symbol of the wand today can remind you that everyone has a special talent that should not be wasted. Recognize the right opportunity to use your trump card and make the most of it.

DILIGENCE

· *Today, the day ahead*—An event could inject some much-needed energy into your daily routine. Don't overthink it—take action and start to reap the rewards.

· *Today, in love*—Listen to your heart, don't let fear stop you from expressing your feelings and taking the first step. Today is a great day for love and new beginnings.

· *Today, at work*—You can finally see the results of your hard work. Your dedication and efforts have paid off and will be acknowledged. Don't be hesitant—take pride in your success and enjoy the moment!

· *Self-reflection*—Now is the perfect time to create something new—whether it be a family or a project—that can bring new purpose to life. You have all the resources you need to make progress and reach your goals.

· *A symbol*—Contemplating the symbol of ivy today can be a potent reminder of renewal and hope. The evergreen plant sprouting from seemingly lifeless wood serves as a reminder that even in uncertain times, you can maintain your confidence and optimism, which can propel you into action and broaden your perspective.

Insecurity · Indifference

The Two of Wands shows a man in stasis, indicating
through his stance the inability or impossibility to choose
and move forward. It may be a stalemate intended or suffered,
a necessary pause, or a blockage to be overcome as soon as possible.

Choose what kind of energy you want to draw from the Two of Wands today:
Insecurity, Conquest, Neutrality

INSECURITY

· *Today, the day ahead*—You might be feeling apathetic and unmotivated today, so it's best to avoid making any rash decisions or trying to force yourself to be in a better mood. Give yourself a break and don't start any activities that require a lot of commitment.

· *Today, in love*—Comprehension is slow, enthusiasm is waning. Neither of you have the drive to decide if you should revive the relationship or part ways. Who will make the first move?

· *Today, at work*—If you're feeling inundated with doubts at work today, it's wise to stay impartial and contemplate seeking an outside evaluation. Don't overload yourself with too much responsibility. Postpone any commitments until you have a clearer grasp of the circumstances. Take all the time you need to carefully think things through.

· *Self-reflection*—Detaching yourself from a situation can be a helpful way to cope, as long as it doesn't lead to complete isolation. If you become too detached, you may start to lose the joy you have for life. To help yourself get back on track, make sure to eat a healthy diet full of fruits and vegetables and take vitamins to help you boost your energy and motivation.

· *A symbol*—Today's symbol for reflection is the globe. The image depicts a man standing and gazing into the distance while holding the world in his hands. The message behind this symbol is that seemingly unreachable goals are, in fact, more possible than you think, and the means to achieve are right in front of you.

CONQUEST

· *Today, the day ahead*—Whatever the situation you find yourself in, have faith in your abilities. You have all the necessary skills to overcome any difficulty and be proud of yourself. Wait with confidence—the time to act is about to come.

· *Today, in love*—Even if your relationship is strong, don't take your partner's happiness for granted. Show them how much you care about them and your relationship. If you're single, there are plenty of opportunities ahead.

· *Today, at work*—If you put in the hard work, you can achieve great success and a highly desirable position. However, it's important to remember that you can't do it all on your own. Don't be afraid to ask for help—it won't weaken your authority.

· *Self-reflection*—What does true wealth mean to you? Is it just having material possessions, or is it something more intangible, like achieving inner peace and moral victory? Take a moment to think about your values, reevaluate your goals, and lower your expectations.

· *A symbol*—Today's symbol for reflection is the conqueror. Who is this man gazing at a distant goal? Is he Alexander the Great or Napoleon, who conquered the world? Whoever he is, he could not have done more, aimed higher, or pushed beyond his limits.

NEUTRALITY

· *Today, the day ahead*—A highly sought-after project may be subject to some delays. There's no need to rush things or blame fate. To avoid any potential issues or miscommunications with those involved, it's best to wait and let things unfold naturally.

· *Today, in love*—If you're looking for love, it's important to take some time to think about what you really want from a relationship and how much you're willing to invest. Don't just focus on physical attraction—try to look beyond the superfluous and get to know the person for who they really are.

· *Today, at work*—Remember the old saying: "When two quarrel, the third rejoices." Keep this in mind at work and try to stay neutral in any disputes. Don't get too involved in matters that don't directly concern you, as it could complicate your life.

· *Self-reflection*—Don't let yourself be overwhelmed by negative or strong emotions. You have all the tools you need to confront any challenge; don't look for complicated solutions. Remember the saying "Less is more."

· *A symbol*—Reflect on the lily and the rose symbols. These two gorgeous flowers represent contrasting ideas: the lily symbolizes purity, while the rose stands for passion. In this card, they are crossed to remind you that balance is key to achieving inner peace.

Success · Forethought

The Three of Wands is a card of optimism and hope. A tall,
strong figure stands on a hill, looking out at the horizon. The sea is
tranquil, and ships sail peacefully across it, signifying peace and prosperity.
This card is a positive omen, suggesting that good things are on the way.

Choose what kind of energy you want to draw from the Three of Wands today:

Optimism, Perfectionism, Solidity

OPTIMISM

· *Today, the day ahead*—Today is a day to be joyful! Nothing can stop you from smiling and looking forward to the future. Put your worries aside and enjoy the moment.

· *Today, in love*—Allow yourself to be carried away by your partner's good vibes and spend a day together doing something fun. You could throw a party with family and friends, book the vacation of your dreams, or even set a wedding date—why not?

· *Today, at work*—The hard work you've put in has laid a strong foundation; now you just have to wait for the rewards of your efforts to come to fruition. Who knows, they could be even bigger than you expect!

· *Self-reflection*—Make the most of this moment of mental clarity and use it to plan for the future and turn your great ideas into tangible projects. Exciting intellectual encounters await you.

· *A symbol*—Reflect on the symbol of ships. The three sailing boats on the horizon represent your thoughts and aspirations. By maintaining focus and navigating through the waves, you can learn to sail with the wind at your back and effortlessly reach your destination.

PERFECTIONISM

· *Today, the day ahead*—Today is the ideal day to hone your skills, sign up for a class, or start studying a new language, art form, or hobby. It's never too late to learn something new!

· *Today, in love*—It seems like everything is going well in your relationship, but do you feel like you could be getting more out of it? Open up to your partner, share your hopes and dreams with them. It's never too late to make a change and spice up your relationship.

· *Today, at work*—It seems like you are not entirely satisfied today; something is missing, you want more from your job. To achieve perfection, you need to be meticulous and pay close attention to detail. This kind of attitude could bring great rewards.

· *Self-reflection*—Dwelling on regrets and remorse isn't productive. Instead, every experience is an opportunity to learn and grow, so it's important to focus on the present and look toward the future.

· *A symbol*—Reflect on the symbolism of the chessboard. The black and white squares represent the highs and lows of life—sometimes we're blessed with good luck, and other times we feel like the universe is against us. But if we stay true to our values, no situation can take us by surprise.

SOLIDITY

· *Today, the day ahead*—Don't be taken aback if everyone comes to you for assistance today—your trustworthiness and dependability are qualities that many admire and are drawn to. If you've set a good example for someone, make sure you don't let them down.

· *Today, in love*—Do you want to win back the person you love? Listen to their fears, reassure them, provide comfort, and let them know that you will always be there for them.

· *Today, at work*—Today is the perfect day to finally tackle those long-postponed tasks or take care of that tedious paperwork. You'll find that everything will go much smoother and faster than usual, and it's not just luck that's on your side—it's your own skill and determination that will get you through. Well done!

· *Self-reflection*—Life's experiences have shaped you, perhaps tested you, but never defeated you. You now have the strength and resilience to approach the future with hope and insight.

· *A symbol*—Today, reflect on the symbolism of the red cloak warmly wrapped around the man. It is a representation of self-esteem and inner strength, providing a sense of security and protection from the elements. No matter what life throws at you, those who are confident in their own value will remain unshaken.

Security · Joy

The Four of Wands symbolizes being appreciated, valued, and safe.
It is a sign of joyous occasions, new connections, and positive experiences.
When it appears, you can feel confident and hopeful about what lies ahead.

Choose what kind of energy you want to draw from the Four of Wands today:

Celebration, Welcome, Harmony

CELEBRATION

· *Today, the day ahead*—Today is a great day to get together with friends, even if there isn't a special occasion. Don't stay cooped up at home feeling down, get out there and have some fun!

· *Today, in love*—Today is a perfect day to celebrate love. If you have a partner, commemorate your first meeting, even if it's not an anniversary. If you're single, open your heart to new encounters. The best way to prepare for something new is to be ready to welcome it!

· *Today, at work*—Focus on doing the tasks that you enjoy the most and that don't tire you out too much. Don't overburden yourself; it's okay to do your duties but take some time to make life easier for yourself. Be friendly and helpful with your colleagues, superiors, employees, and customers. You'll reap the rewards of your kindness soon enough.

· *Self-reflection*—Today is the perfect day to embrace life, get to know new people, and look ahead with enthusiasm and interest. Have you considered joining a gym or a dance class? It would be beneficial for both your physical and mental health, plus you'd make some new friends.

· *A symbol*—Today, reflect on the symbol of the dancers. Those vibrant figures dancing in the background, with garlands of flowers in their hands, symbolize the wonderful surprises that life has in store for you. No matter what difficulties you may be facing, there is always something to be grateful for.

WELCOME

· *Today, the day ahead*—Smiling is contagious, and it can really make a difference in how people interact with you. When you have an optimistic outlook, it can be felt by those around you. Show your appreciation for the little things in life, and more will come your way. Why not take the time to catch up with an old friend you haven't seen in a while?

· *Today, in love*—Should any issues of jealousy or disagreement with your loved one have occurred in the past, they should now have been resolved and feel like a distant memory. Today is a day of peace for families, harmony for couples, and promise for those seeking love.

· *Today, at work*—Today is an especially good day to make deals and form partnerships. At work, don't turn down an offer to join a business or organization, as it could benefit you in many ways.

· *Self-reflection*—To rejuvenate and prepare yourself for the days ahead, consider chilling out and spending a day in the countryside surrounded by flowers and animals. Take time to unwind, breathe in the fresh air, and absorb the peaceful surroundings.

· *A symbol*—Reflecting on the symbol of the flowers today can remind you of the celebration of life, the fertility of nature, and the return of spring. Every stage of life has its own beauty, and it is never too late to find joy and happiness.

HARMONY

· *Today, the day ahead*—It's time to celebrate your accomplishments and savor life! But don't forget that success is often a team effort. Show your gratitude to those who have supported you and give credit to those who have helped you along the way. Good things are on the horizon!

· *Today, in love*—True love is like a cozy hearth at home, providing warmth, nourishment, and comfort. Today is the perfect day to start making plans for the future, searching for a place to call home, and considering living together or tying the knot. Because let's face it, what's the point of being in a relationship if you can't share your life with each other?

· *Today, at work*—Today is a special day at work as a project you've been invested in for a long time may finally come to fruition. You can now share your success and accomplishments with those close to you. It's a particularly auspicious day for work groups and teams.

· *Self-reflection*—Science tells us that humans are social creatures and cannot reach true inner peace unless they have positive relationships with their fellow human beings. Today, take a moment to reflect on how you interact with others. Are you open to listening and understanding their perspectives? Do you have meaningful relationships with your friends, and if so, what do you do to show them how much you care?

· *A symbol*—Today, the castle is a symbol to reflect on. It stands for success, stability, and protection. Everyone has a special place, be it real or imagined, where they can find solace and peace away from the hustle and bustle of life and enjoy their own privacy. It doesn't have to be grand or luxurious; the important thing is that it has personal value to you.

Efforts · Courage

The Five of Wands tells us about the courage it takes to face life's trials. When this card appears, you are spurred to demonstrate your ability to evolve and solve problems. Roll up your sleeves and throw yourself into the fray!

Choose what kind of energy you want to draw from the Five of Wands today:

Competition, Crisis, Conflict

COMPETITION

· *Today, the day ahead*—Today is the perfect day to get some exercise, whether it's a light workout or a more intense one. If you're playing a sport competitively, you have a great chance of winning.

· *Today, in love*—You may feel challenged in your relationship. Do you feel like you need to prove something to your partner, or is there someone else you feel like you have to compete with to win their affection? Whatever the case, always stay true to yourself. Respect yourself above all else.

· *Today, at work*—It's time to prove yourself and show everyone what you're capable of. Don't be afraid to compete with your colleagues at work, but remember that it's not about winning, it's about showing that you can take risks and stand your ground. Don't take shortcuts—be honest and do your best.

· *Self-reflection*—You have a brave hero inside you that won't give up no matter what challenges you face. Don't hold it back; let it out and you'll be surprised at what you can do.

· *A symbol*—Today's symbol to reflect on is the fighters. The card depicts boys engaged in a stick fight without harming each other. They are energetically competing to demonstrate their strength. This symbolizes the potential you have to show your talents when faced with a difficult situation and you are called to take action.

CRISIS

· *Today, the day ahead*—You may struggle to achieve what you set out to do. Reach out to your close friends or people you trust for help; you'll be sure to return the favor without any delay tomorrow.

· *Today, in love*—When speaking to the person you love, be mindful of your words. Choose them carefully so as not to hurt their feelings. Show your support and understanding with your actions and use your diplomatic skills to make sure your message is heard.

· *Today, at work*—This day could be particularly stressful, with too many commitments, demands, and deadlines to meet. To get through it, rely on your most hardworking and cooperative colleagues; working together as a team will be the key to success.

· *Self-reflection*—If you want to reach your full potential, you need to be comfortable interacting with others and not be afraid of confrontation. Remember, not everyone is an adversary and it's important to not judge others if you don't want to be judged yourself.

· *A symbol*—Reflect on the symbol of quarreling. Criticisms, arguments, and even jokes can be really hurtful, especially when they come from people you care about. And yet, while it's important to be sensitive, constructive criticism can be essential for growth and improvement.

CONFLICT

· *Today, the day ahead*—Today, conflicts with the people around you may cause some tension and disrupt your peace of mind. If you express your opinion, it could bring up some unresolved issues and give you the opportunity to resolve them. This could even improve your relationships with them in the long run.

· *Today, in love*—Every now and then, even the most long-term and devoted couples will have disagreements. It's not right for only one of them to back down; both should be able to express their opinions and make their case. The key is to always maintain respect for each other.

· *Today, at work*—If you find yourself in the middle of a disagreement between two colleagues at work, it's crucial to remain calm and impartial. Avoid taking sides; instead, focus on facilitating a dialogue between the parties involved to restore a constructive atmosphere.

· *Self-reflection*—We are all reflections of each other, projecting our own strengths and weaknesses onto others. To better understand your own strengths, it can be helpful to reflect on the qualities you admire in the people you look up to. Conversely, to gain insight into your own weaknesses, it can be illuminating to examine the traits you criticize in others.

· *A symbol*—Today, take a moment to reflect on the symbol of boys playing a lively game, dressed in colorful and joyful outfits. This image embodies the courage to take risks and be vulnerable, regardless of age. Facing life's challenges takes self-confidence, and embracing our inner childlike sense of play can be a powerful way to nurture that confidence.

Happy Event · Victory

The Six of Wands represents positive progress and happy events.
A returning hero is cheered and celebrated by admirers after
his unexpected but well-deserved victories.

Choose what kind of energy you want to draw from the Six of Wands today:

Success, Resoluteness, Recognition

SUCCESS

· *Today, the day ahead*—The enthusiasm you show today could be inspiring to those around you, but it could also be misinterpreted as arrogance. Try to stay humble.

· *Today, in love*—Let go of any hesitation and express your feelings today—you may be surprised by the response. A simple, heartfelt gift can make a big impact.

· *Today, at work*—Your strategies and action plans are paying off and you will soon be rewarded for your hard work, even if some of your competitors may be envious. Get ready, your success will undoubtedly make you the talk of the town.

· *Self-reflection*—Now that the conflict with someone or within yourself is resolved, you can finally enjoy inner peace. Before you share your plans with anyone, make sure they are fully formed and that your intentions have become concrete facts.

· *A symbol*—Reflecting on the symbol of the laurel wreath serves as a reminder of victory and achievement. Striving for success requires courage and determination, and it also means being willing to accept defeat. Consider asking yourself, how ready are you to face the challenges of competition?

RESOLUTENESS

· *Today, the day ahead*—If you need clarity today, consider the person who has been a major source of guidance for you: what would they do in your shoes? If possible, reach out to them directly.

· *Today, in love*—Love is not a competition; show your appreciation for your partner and celebrate their success and achievements.

· *Today, at work*—Having an optimistic attitude at work can be beneficial in creating many opportunities. However, it's important not to get ahead of yourself and to stay focused until the goal is reached.

· *Self-reflection*—If you're reflecting on some of your past decisions today, it's a sign that you're growing, and your soul is evolving. Don't be too hard on yourself—no need for guilt. You're a fighter, and it's okay to stumble every now and then. Just pick yourself up and keep going!

· *A symbol*—Reflecting on the symbol of the garland trophy can be a reminder that life is like a tournament. It takes good aim to hit the goal, determination to reach it, and humility to sustain it.

RECOGNITION

· *Today, the day ahead*—All of the things that have been weighing you down and making you feel exhausted will be taken care of quickly. Don't just put it down to luck; it's all because of your efforts that things are finally going in the right direction. Keep up the good work!

· *Today, in love*—If you're in love, there's plenty to be happy about. If you're in a relationship, you and your partner can grow even closer; if you're single, you'll soon find someone special.

· *Today, at work*—It may be a challenging period for many at work, but not for you. Stay focused on your goals, stay positive, and don't let any obstacles stand in your way. Things will soon be looking up.

· *Self-reflection*—If you have always been generous in helping others, you should be proud of yourself. Don't feel the need to be recognized by others, but if you are, accept it with humility. This will make you even more admirable.

· *A symbol*—Today, reflect on the symbol of the white horse. This majestic creature, with its proud, snow-white coat and festive harness, symbolizes nobility of spirit—the quality of one who stands up for great causes, regardless of their wealth or social standing.

Tenacity · Courage

The Seven of Wands is a reminder of courage and strength,
showing that you have the power to face any enemy,
challenge, or difficulty that comes your way.

Choose what kind of energy you want to draw from the Seven of Wands today:
Facing Challenges, Courage, Self-Affirmation

FACING CHALLENGES

· *Today, the day ahead*—Today, no matter what challenge you're facing, arm yourself with courage and take it head-on. Don't procrastinate, and don't let anyone take away your rights. Stand up for yourself and don't back down!

· *Today, in love*—You and your partner have been through so much together, and nothing can prevent you from achieving your joy. Those who love each other deeply don't pay attention to what other people think and keep pushing forward.

· *Today, at work*—It's time to take charge at work and face any difficult situations directly. Don't be afraid to stand up to those who are causing trouble, whether it's a colleague or a superior. Don't let yourself be intimidated—it's time to show what you're capable of.

· *Self-reflection*—Ignoring problems won't bring you peace of mind. Trying to escape them with harmful behaviors like drinking or taking drugs can only pushes you closer to the brink. The only way to find serenity is to face your challenges and do whatever it takes to overcome them.

· *A symbol*—Reflect on the symbol of the chasm. This card portrays a lone figure vulnerable to the aggression of sticks that could lead to him tipping over and plunging into the abyss. Remember, when facing obstacles, having the conviction that you are in the right will give you the strength to overcome any challenge or opponent.

COURAGE

· *Today, the day ahead*—It's true that you won't always get what you want right away; sometimes you have to work hard and persevere to achieve your goals. So don't give up, even when the going gets tough.

· *Today, in love*—If you find yourself in a situation where you need to defend your loved one, either by speaking up or taking action, be brave and show your support. Your courage will make you a hero in their eyes and earn their admiration.

· *Today, at work*—There's a lot of competition in the workplace. Today you'll have to fight to keep the position you've worked so hard for. Show your strength and don't lose your self-belief.

· *Self-reflection*—It's never too late to overcome struggles like addictions, obsessions, and fears. There's always a chance for redemption. All you need is some self-love and inner strength to make it happen.

· *A symbol*—Reflect on the symbol of the man's proud facial expression. Recognize his strength and determination to fight for what is right. Let this serve as a reminder that you too possess a fighting spirit within you.

SELF-AFFIRMATION

· *Today, the day ahead*—You might receive some criticism today, but don't worry, you have the ability to defend yourself. Don't let the jealousy of others affect you; you are unbeatable. Don't waste your time on people who don't acknowledge your efforts.

· *Today, in love*—With your partner, try to be more open and less guarded. Listen to what they have to say and use your intuition to decide if it is helpful advice or just baseless accusations. Don't let yourself get drawn into a power struggle—the heart is not meant for that.

· *Today, at work*—Taking an assertive stance can be the key to success. With so much competition, you have the upper hand. Make sure you come out on top!

· *Self-reflection*—Sometimes it may seem like the universe is conspiring against you. While it may be easier to go with the flow during such times, there may also be instances where it's simply not an option. Defending your ideas vigorously and remaining true to yourself is a sign of strength of character and dignity.

· *A symbol*—Today's symbol to reflect on is the green tunic. This garment symbolizes the values and principles you believe in, and your commitment to staying true to yourself, no matter what other people may say or think.

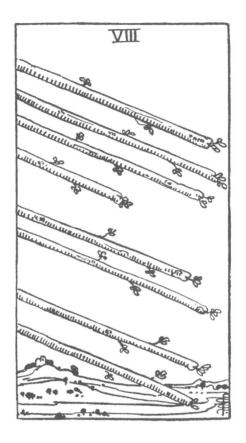

Good News · Interesting Revelations

The Eight of Wands tells you that there is something new in the air: a change, perhaps, or a nice surprise that—perhaps very soon—will become apparent.

Choose what kind of energy you want to draw from the Eight of Wands today:

Surprise, Sudden Change, Energy

SURPRISE

· *Today, the day ahead*—Go look in your mailbox; you might get some exciting news that could completely change your plans. Things will move quickly, but it will be a positive change.

· *Today, in love*—Unexpected events can bring new energy and excitement into a couple's life, as long as both partners are on board with it. For singles, it's a good idea to take advantage of invitations and proposals that come through email or phone to meet new people and explore new opportunities.

· *Today, at work*—Today, the obstacle that has been impeding your progress at work will finally be resolved, allowing for a smoother path forward. Projects may have a promising start and advance rapidly, so make sure to seize the opportunity.

· *Self-reflection*—Today presents the ideal chance to set aside your worries and face the future with hope. If possible, consider taking a break outdoors in nature to recharge your batteries.

· *A symbol*—Take a moment to meditate on the image of a stream. Imagine a crystal-clear stream running through a verdant plain, and let it serve as a reminder that the energy of life exists within us all and will always find a way to flow and channel its power.

SUDDEN CHANGE

· *Today, the day ahead*—That's right, the most profound changes come from within, but if you don't take steps to make your dreams a reality, you won't be able to alter your fate. So take action and be enthusiastic about the opportunities that come your way today.

· *Today, in love*—A refreshing, spring-like breeze is blowing, signaling a change in the air and a new awakening of the senses.

· *Today, at work*—Today at work, it's important to act quickly and skillfully. If you want to avoid making any mistakes, you'll need to stay focused and be extra careful.

· *Self-reflection*—Today is your chance to take control of your destiny. Don't be afraid of change; seize the opportunity and take the plunge! Dare to be bold and see where it takes you.

· *A symbol*—Today, meditate on the symbol of the wind. The wands are propelled by an invisible yet powerful force, just like willpower—the determination of those who are driven to reach their goals, no matter what obstacles they face.

ENERGY

· *Today, the day ahead*—Today is the perfect time to head outside and get some exercise. If you're feeling a bit hesitant, don't worry—just take that first step and you will soon find yourself filled with energy and enthusiasm. Lace up your sneakers and get out there!

· *Today, in love*—It's time to start making plans. Have you been thinking about moving in together? Before buying new property, consider whether renovating the one you already live in might be a good alternative. If you are single, why not take a trip and see if you meet someone special along the way?

· *Today, at work*—If you're feeling like things at work could change soon, consider whether that fits in with your plans. Is it worth staying or would it be better to look for something new? Talk to people you trust to get their opinion.

· *Self-reflection*—The gentle caress of the wind rustling through the trees, the sweet melody of birdsong, the earthy aroma of moss, and the breathtaking beauty of blooming buds—this is what could bring you joy today.

· *A symbol*—Reflect on the symbol of the sprout, a symbol of what is called *viriditas*—the magical life-giving force of Mother Nature. It is a reminder of her power to bring life to her creatures, and to restore life to places where it has been consumed.

NINE OF WANDS

Protection · Solidity

The Nine of Wands suggests the need, whether real or imagined,
to protect yourself. It can indicate a sense of caution and suspicion,
but also of good health as well as mental and physical strength.

Choose what kind of energy you want to draw from the Nine of Wands today:
Guard, Support, Stability

GUARD

· *Today, the day ahead*—Are you feeling a bit on the defensive side today? It looks like you're taking every comment very personally. Is something causing you to feel threatened, or is this stemming from old wounds? Don't be too quick to push people away.

· *Today, in love*—If you want to have a truly intimate and understanding relationship with your partner, it's important to let your guard down. It can be hard to open up if you've been hurt in the past, but it's important to not let those experiences cloud your current relationship.

· *Today, at work*—The work environment is quite insular; everyone is focused on their own tasks, and it can be difficult to rely on the help of others. However, there must be someone you can work with harmoniously—take a good look around and see who you can trust.

· *Self-reflection*—Have you considered that your reserved demeanor may be contributing to people's unapproachable attitude toward you? If you try to be more open and friendly, it could make a significant difference right away.

· *A symbol*—Today's symbol for contemplation is the barrier. Notice the sticks behind the man are arranged like a wall, symbolizing the boundaries you set between yourself and others. While boundaries are essential for self-preservation, they can also hinder your ability to connect.

SUPPORT

· *Today, the day ahead*—You're almost there! You've done the hard work, but don't let your guard down yet. Just a bit more patience and you'll be able to celebrate your success!

· *Today, in love*—Your partner has been through a lot, and some experiences may have left scars that you do not fully comprehend. It's important to be there for your other half and offer support. Your love can provide the strength and nourishment needed to move forward.

· *Today, at work*—You may encounter some minor challenges at work today. Worry not! You have the skills and knowledge to overcome them.

· *Self-reflection*—Life has taught you that you must strive to get what you want and that you should never let your guard down, or you may lose what you have worked hard for. You are now strong and resilient, but don't forget that you don't have to do everything alone. If there is someone you can rely on, don't hesitate to ask for their help.

· *A symbol*—Today's symbol for reflection is the stick. In this context, it represents physical support, much like a crutch for an elderly or injured person. It serves as a reminder of the things in life that provide stability and prevent us from falling.

SOLIDITY

· *Today, the day ahead*—This card encourages you to have faith in your talents and capabilities, of which there are many, but it also reminds you not to be too insular. Don't push yourself too hard; be content with what you have in the present.

· *Today, in love*—If you're in a relationship, you can overcome any challenges by working together with your partner. If you're single, it may be best to take some time to heal from past wounds before pursuing a new relationship.

· *Today, at work*—You've earned everything you have through hard work and dedication. Your efforts will soon bear fruit. Take a moment to relax and trust your coworkers. For those who participate in competitive sports, victories and satisfaction are in sight.

· *Self-reflection*—Not all unforeseen events are necessarily bad. Some happen to teach us valuable lessons in life, while others are merely trivialities that are best not dwelled upon too much.

· *A symbol*—Today's symbol for reflection is the head bandage. In Japanese culture, the hachimaki is a cloth headband worn to represent commitment, perseverance, and dedication to a cause or mission. The wearer strives to overcome any obstacle to achieve their goals.

Excessive Burdens and Expectations

The Ten of Wands depicts a man who is clearly exerting excessive effort. This card advises against taking on an overwhelming amount of burdens and responsibilities.

Choose what kind of energy you want to draw from the Ten of Wands today:

Burden, Responsibility, Fatigue

BURDEN

· *Today, the day ahead*—Be mindful not to take on too many commitments today, as you may become overwhelmed and struggle to manage them all effectively. It's best to prioritize essential tasks and focus on completing those to the best of your ability. Also, a word of caution: watch out for muscle strains.

· *Today, in love*—If your relationship has hit a rough patch, it may not be solely your or your partner's responsibility, but rather the challenges that you are both facing. Through open communication and dialogue, you can work toward rebuilding emotional intimacy and a stronger bond.

· *Today, at work*—The workload is quite overwhelming! Is this just for today or is it like this every day? If it's a recurring issue, consider delegating some tasks to others to alleviate the stress. If you feel like you can't do everything, just focus on completing something.

· *Self-reflection*—While taking on responsibilities is undoubtedly a sign of maturity, if you find yourself overwhelmed and feeling weighed down, it's a sign that you're pushing yourself too hard. It's important to recognize that you can't handle everything alone, and it's okay to ask for help.

· *A symbol*—The symbol to reflect on today is timber. The man carrying a heavy load of wood represents the commitments that you take on in life. While some of these commitments may be unavoidable, many of them can be excessive and difficult to manage. Remember to take it easy and not overload yourself.

RESPONSIBILITY

· *Today, the day ahead*—It seems that the time has come for you to reap what you have sown, for better or for worse. Are you ready to take responsibility for your choices and face the consequences of your actions?

· *Today, in love*—If you're single, don't rush into the search for love. Dating too many people can be overwhelming, so take your time to find someone who is truly compatible with you and what you're looking for in a relationship. If you're already in a relationship, show your partner some support today.

· *Today, at work*—If you want to meet your deadlines at work, it's important to optimize your time. Avoid distractions and stay focused to avoid not achieving as much as you would have hoped for by the end of the day.

· *Self-reflection*—If you're feeling oppressed or stuck in a situation that seems unsolvable, take a moment to let things unfold naturally. It's not about giving up, but rather acknowledging that you can't control everything.

· *A symbol*—Today's symbol for reflection is the village. The houses appearing on the horizon represent distant goals. If you take on too many commitments, you may lose sight of the main objective and waste the energy required to achieve it.

FATIGUE

· *Today, the day ahead*—Brace yourself for a hectic day ahead! You'll likely be running around a lot, responding to multiple requests, and trying to meet tight deadlines. It could even be a good day to do some deep cleaning around the house. Just be mindful not to take on too much or your back and your mind will suffer.

· *Today, in love*—If there have been some issues between you and your partner, it may be time to put your pride aside and let go of any resentments. Do you still recall the dreams you had together? You may both be wondering what happened to them or if they still exist somewhere deep in your hearts.

· *Today, at work*—At work, everything is on your shoulders, especially if you're a craftsperson. Your business might be booming, but stress will inevitably take its toll. Try to manage your energy levels so you don't get too exhausted.

· *Self-reflection*—Being humble doesn't always mean keeping your head down. It means accepting earned credit without boasting about it. If someone tends to take advantage of your helpfulness, it's essential to learn to stand up for yourself and not allow them to exploit you.

· *A symbol*—Today, reflect on the bent back. Sometimes life's challenges can bend you out of shape. To lift your head up again, both physical and psychological support can be helpful—you can't always go it alone.

PAGE OF WANDS

Motivation · Excitement

The Page of Wands symbolizes opportunities from the outside world that may come to a young person or an enthusiastic seeker. It suggests exciting proposals that can inject new life into stagnant situations.

Choose what kind of energy you want to draw from the Page of Wands today: **Enthusiasm, Straightforwardness, Creative Spark**

ENTHUSIASM

· *Today, the day ahead*—If a friend suggests something different today, don't turn down their offer! Embrace the opportunity and get involved. You never know what kind of fantastic adventure or new interests you might discover.

· *Today, in love*—You might come across an exciting opportunity that can breathe new life into your relationship, like a trip or adventure. Don't miss out on it! Who knows, you might even rediscover a passion you thought you had lost. So go for it!

· *Today, at work*—You might receive a tempting offer at work today. But before you jump on it, take a moment to consider all the potential consequences that come with your decision. Don't let your enthusiasm cloud your judgment—take a step back and think it through carefully.

· *Self-reflection*—Even if you're usually a cautious person or not easily swayed by enthusiasm, today might bring an event that challenges your certainties. Do you have the courage to face something new? As the saying goes, "No risk, no gain." So, are you willing to take a chance and see what happens?

· *A symbol*—Today, the symbol to reflect on is the flame. Take note of the Page's headgear—it resembles a helmet or a hat adorned with a plume that could be a red feather or a flame. This represents enthusiasm—the spark that ignites in your soul whenever life presents you with a new opportunity. It's up to you to fuel that flame or let it fizzle out.

STRAIGHTFORWARDNESS

· *Today, the day ahead*—If you're young, this card suggests that today, with a bit of boldness, you can overcome situations that have been stagnant. If you're not so young anymore, it may mean that you'll approach the day with the spirit of a 20-year-old.

· *Today, in love*—If you were presented with an indecent proposal, how would you respond? Would you jump at the chance or turn it down gracefully? An exciting opportunity can rekindle your passion for life but be careful not to get burned!

· *Today, at work*—While you're at work today, take a moment to reflect on how much you're willing to do to advance your career or increase your salary. Would you consider using unethical methods to satisfy your ambition? Additionally, consider how your reputation stands currently.

· *Self-reflection*—Perhaps it's time to seek external inspiration to inject some excitement back into your daily routine. Be open to new experiences, consider proposals from friends, and allow yourself some small breaks from your usual routines. In other words, break away from your typical patterns!

· *A symbol*—Today, take some time to reflect on the symbol of the embroidered robe. The Page's incredibly sophisticated garment serves as a reminder that having a passion for life is a talent. Those who are unable to take risks every now and then are more likely to age prematurely.

CREATIVE SPARK

· *Today, the day ahead*—Your creative energy is in full flow today. If you don't have a specific plan, why not tackle some projects that you've been putting off due to procrastination, or start something new altogether? Don't stress about making it perfect; instead, concentrate on enjoying the process.

· *Today, in love*—There's an undeniable sense of yearning for a passionate romance or a shared pursuit of building something significant between you and your partner. However, the idea of starting a family may still be a distant goal. Taking that leap requires a sense of rootedness, certainty, and maturity.

· *Today, at work*—Today presents an opportunity for you to exhibit and make use of your talents. When it comes to work, there's no obstacle you can't confront and overcome, no objective that's beyond your reach. Ignore those who belittle your motives and forge ahead confidently.

· *Self-reflection*—This card serves as a reminder that if you've lost track of your priorities and stumbled in various aspects of your life, it's time to leave the past behind and approach the future with renewed enthusiasm. Engaging in artistic activities is highly recommended.

· *A symbol*—Today, take some time to reflect on the symbol of the pyramids. In this card, they represent human ambition, as for the pharaohs they were considered the means of conquering the afterlife. If you have the ability to harness your talents and possess strong willpower, you can go far and attain your most coveted aspirations.

Value · Ardor

The Knight of Wands symbolizes energy flowing in a particular direction. The atmosphere is warm and passionate, but also impatient and somewhat deceptive.

Choose what kind of energy you want to draw from the Knight of Wands today:

Impatience, Audacity, Drive

IMPATIENCE

· *Today, the day ahead*—Today, you might feel tied down by your routine: you crave fun, new places, and meeting people—in short, you need a vacation. However, it's best to hold off on booking your trip; haste is not a wise decision.

· *Today, in love*—If you're feeling the heat of love, take a moment to consider if it's a true flame of passion or just a passing spark. Make sure to communicate your intentions to your partner, or you could end up getting burned.

· *Today, at work*—If you're feeling overwhelmed at work, try to take a step back and remember that rushing through tasks can lead to mistakes. Take your time and stay focused on the task at hand.

· *Self-reflection*—Have you considered the potential consequences of making a big change in your life, or do you just need a break? Taking some time to reflect on the possible outcomes of your decisions can help you make the best choice.

· *A symbol*—Reflect on the symbol of the plume. The Page has become a Knight, his helmet is now blazing with enthusiasm, and his eagerness is quickly turning into impatience. Keep impulsiveness under control.

AUDACITY

· *Today, the day ahead*—Today is the perfect day to express yourself and show the world what you stand for. You have the energy, the charisma, and the passion to fight for your rights and beliefs. Your enthusiasm has the power to inspire and mobilize others.

· *Today, in love*—There's a promise of passion and intensity for both couples and singles alike. If you receive an enticing offer or proposition, consider letting yourself indulge in the moment, just this once. Allow your senses to take over and fully experience the heat of the moment.

· *Today, at work*—Some significant changes are on the horizon at work, such as role changes or transfers. Your ability to navigate these changes will largely depend on how resilient and adaptable you appear. This is your chance to showcase your skills and demonstrate what you're capable of.

· *Self-reflection*—You may be going through a period of significant personal growth and renewal. To help restore focus and inner peace, consider practicing breathing exercises or engaging in physical activity that allows you to release built-up energy. There's no greater gift you can give yourself than the gift of travel.

· *A symbol*—Contemplate the symbol of the pyramids. These ancient tombs of the pharaohs are considered one of the wonders of the world, and they represent the treasures that lie buried within our own souls. Only those who possess the courage to delve deep and confront the unknown can unearth these treasures.

DRIVE

· *Today, the day ahead*—Today, motivation is at an all-time high. With focus and preparedness, you can accomplish your goals in record time. There's nothing that can hold you back—if you set your mind to it, you can impress both yourself and those around you. The moment for action has arrived.

· *Today, in love*—Have you ever dreamed of meeting a romantic Prince Charming? What if, instead, you encountered a captivating person who could transform your life and shake up your worldview? A charismatic Knight of Wands could capture your heart, and the possibilities are endless. Such an experience could be truly life changing.

· *Today, at work*—A forthcoming change at work may take everyone by surprise, leaving some feeling unprepared and disheartened. It's possible that tensions may rise, and conflicts may occur. While it's important to avoid arguments and fights, it's equally important to make your voice heard.

· *Self-reflection*—You have a remarkable ability to face life's challenges with courage and determination, no matter how difficult they may be. Yet, beneath your seemingly impenetrable exterior, there may be underlying fears and insecurities. It's important not to be evasive with your friends and to confide in them when you need support.

· *A symbol*—Today's symbol to reflect upon is the prancing horse. The image portrays a rider on a spirited horse that is rearing up on its hind legs, suggesting that it may not be fully tamed. However, the rider remains firmly in the saddle, undeterred by the horse's sudden movements. This powerful image serves as a reminder that by staying true to your principles and remaining focused on your goals, you can withstand any unexpected obstacles that come your way.

Self-Confidence · Courage · Joy of Living

The Queen of Wands represents recognizing your own self-worth and inspiring yourself and others. It also represents courage and sex appeal.

Choose what kind of energy you want to draw from the Queen of Wands today:

Self-Esteem, Vitality, Resourcefulness

SELF-ESTEEM

· *Today, the day ahead*—Your charm and charisma will undoubtedly help you gain the recognition you deserve when presenting your ideas and proposals. Nothing can stand in the way of your positive attitude today.

· *Today, in love*—Romantically, you may find yourself captivated by an incredibly sensual person. To win them over, try unleashing your resourcefulness or perhaps consider giving them a thoughtful gift like a flower.

· *Today, at work*—At work, if you draw the Queen of Wands card, it's a sign of leadership. Whether you're in a position of authority or not, assert yourself and get your colleagues excited about your projects. If your boss is the one embodying the Queen of Wands, make sure to get involved in their innovative ideas.

· *Self-reflection*—You shouldn't settle for the mundane routine today. Instead, seek out an exhilarating and unforgettable experience that will take your breath away and get your adrenaline pumping, something that is uniquely yours and no one else's. However, it's important to exercise a bit of patience.

· *A symbol*—The symbol to reflect on today is the cat. Few creatures embody self-assuredness quite like a cat. Despite their small and adorable appearance, they always maintain a sense of ferocity and confidence.

VITALITY

· *Today, the day ahead*—Today is not the time to be idle. Get outside and take advantage of the beauty of nature. Spend some time with people who bring you joy.

· *Today, in love*—You may not realize it, but your charm is something that others can sense and appreciate. Your natural sweetness and positive attitude are what make you shine in the eyes of those around you, so there's no need to try too hard or dress up just to impress.

· *Today, at work*—Today is a great day for business. Take the advice of someone with a lot of experience, especially if it's a woman, and believe firmly in your abilities. It's an extremely profitable day for artists as well.

· *Self-reflection*—A period of great inner renewal, both mentally and spiritually, is on the horizon. Look toward the future with optimism, confidence, and heightened awareness. If possible, practice some mindfulness exercises to aid in this process.

· *A symbol*—The symbol to reflect on today is the sunflower. What flower could better represent energy, vibrancy, and the joy of life? By staying true to your ideals (like the sun) and accumulating experiences (like seeds), success in life is sure to come.

RESOURCEFULNESS

· *Today, the day ahead*—Why do you feel the need to always seek advice and approval from others? You are strong and capable and can succeed on your own. Remember the saying, "If you want a job done well, do it yourself."

· *Today, in love*—If you want to win over someone special all you have to do is involve them in an exciting and somewhat crazy activity. This will give you such an irresistible appeal, they won't be able to turn you down.

· *Today, at work*—If you're looking to advance your career, showcase your dependability and worth to your superiors. However, if you aspire to be a leader or have an entrepreneurial mindset, it may be the right time to venture out on your own.

· *Self-reflection*—Your love for life frequently prompts you to push your limits and engage in daring and challenging activities. While it's great to explore new experiences, make sure to stay grounded and prioritize your health and safety.

· *A symbol*—Today's symbol for contemplation is the throne with lions. This throne, resembling the one belonging to the goddess Cybele, lady of the forest and wild creatures, represents the powerful and often opposing forces of creation and destruction found in nature.

Willpower · Decision-Making Power

The King of Wands symbolizes an individual of significant value and unwavering resolve, who is always prepared to take decisive and brave action both for himself and for others.

Choose what kind of energy you want to draw from the King of Wands today:

Worth, Readiness, Honesty

WORTH

· *Today, the day ahead*—It looks like the day is going to be quite busy, so you'll have to buckle down and demonstrate your capabilities. Be prepared to move quickly and efficiently to achieve your objective in no time.

· *Today, in love*—If you're feeling up for some adventure, keep in mind that your charm and sex appeal are likely to attract attention. If you're in a relationship, relish the harmonious and affectionate atmosphere within your family and cherish the admiration that your partner has for you.

· *Today, at work*—Today is a great day for business. It's best to take charge and deal with any problems before they get out of hand. There's also potential for a burst of creativity in creative projects, and you may get unexpected help from a man.

· *Self-reflection*—Today would be an ideal day to focus on maintaining your muscular and skeletal health, particularly if you are getting a bit older. Have you considered incorporating some postural exercises into your routine?

· *A symbol*—Today, the salamander is a symbol to reflect on. This animal, associated with the element of fire and highly esteemed by alchemists, symbolizes the capacity to adapt to unexpected circumstances and to thrive in the toughest of conditions.

READINESS

· *Today, the day ahead*—You have so much energy and enthusiasm that you can't just let it go to waste. Today is the perfect day to finally take on that task you've been putting off—why not involve some friends and make it a group effort? You won't regret it!

· *Today, in love*—You may be drawn to someone who is independent, vivacious, and confident. If you feel intimidated by them, why not take a chance and make the first move? You never know, you might just be able to win them over!

· *Today, at work*—At work, this card encourages you to take the initiative and be a leader. Don't wait around for instructions; take action and get things done.

· *Self-reflection*—It's the ideal day to get outside and soak up some sunshine. Don't forget to stock up on your vitamin D, which is great for your bones and keeps your muscles functioning properly. But don't forget to bring your sunglasses and sunscreen too!

· *A symbol*—The symbol that you should contemplate today is the snapshot. Observe the posture of the King in the image—he appears to be on the brink of standing up at any given moment. Despite his seated position on the throne, the King is poised and prepared to take action and engage with his subjects. He represents quick-wittedness and sharp reflexes.

HONESTY

· *Today, the day ahead*—This card is encouraging you to take the initiative and demonstrate your ambition. Don't let yourself be lazy or procrastinate—if you don't have the motivation to get started, reach out to someone who can help you find the strength.

· *Today, in love*—The chemistry and attraction between you and the person you desire is undeniable, with a tangible erotic tension brewing between you. While this may lead to the ignition of passion and desire, if you're currently in a committed relationship, it's important to remain loyal and resist temptation before things get out of hand. Keep in mind that an attractive man may either pique your interest or pose as a love rival.

· *Today, at work*—It may be necessary for you to adopt a more serious and authoritative demeanor than usual. It's essential to establish your boundaries and make it clear that you won't tolerate being pushed around. Those who recognize and value your capabilities and worth will undoubtedly support you.

· *Self-reflection*—Honesty starts within. If you don't take the time to know yourself and be honest with yourself, you can't expect to have meaningful and genuine relationships with others. The King is a representation of this truth.

· *A symbol*—Today, reflect on the symbol of the scepter. This ruler's scepter is a wand with lush green sprouts growing from it, symbolizing creative power, artistic flair, and vitality.

Lucidity · Knowledge

The Ace of Swords symbolizes knowledge, the power of the mind,
and the ability to make informed and wise decisions. It encourages you
to think clearly and to use your intellect to find solutions.

Choose what kind of energy you want to draw from the Ace of Swords today:
Lucidity, New Ideas, Decision-Making

LUCIDITY

· *Today, the day ahead*—If you can stay calm and level-headed today, you can find a great solution to a problem that has been bothering you for a while. Take a deep breath, focus, and then act. Keep your thoughts in the present moment.

· *Today, in love*—While might be uncomfortable to have this conversation, it is important to figure out if you and your partner need to start fresh or if it's time to move on. Clarifying the details of your relationship now will help you make the best decision for both of you.

· *Today, at work*—Today is a great day to embark on a new endeavor at work, whether it's a business venture or a project. However, before diving in too deep, it's crucial to carefully plan out each step and attend to all the necessary details to avoid becoming overwhelmed by the finer intricacies.

· *Self-reflection*—If you can take a step back and not let your emotions take over, you can tackle any challenge. Before responding to a provocation, take a moment to count to ten and consider your response.

· *A symbol*—Today, reflect on the symbol of the golden crown. Adorned with gems and evergreens, this crown symbolizes concentration, mental clarity, and the sharpness of a brilliant intellect.

NEW IDEAS

· *Today, the day ahead*—No way will you stand for injustice. Even if you don't think of yourself as a hero, when your core values are violated, you become enraged. Don't be afraid to speak up and defend yourself—your words are powerful.

· *Today, in love*—Today, try to approach your partner's proposals and initiatives with curiosity and interest. This can inject a fresh sense of energy and vitality into your relationship.

· *Today, at work*—Your ideas are likely to be well received in the work environment today, so it's a good opportunity to take advantage of that if you're looking to shake up the internal dynamics. The Arcanum is urging you to share everything you're thinking and remember that you have the power to influence the situation.

· *Self-reflection*—Don't give away your ideas to those who don't recognize their value; carefully choose who to trust and make sure to clear up any misunderstandings or false assumptions with those who are worthy of your friendship.

· *A symbol*—The symbol of the mountains can be seen as a metaphor for the highest levels of intellect. The lofty peaks in the background of the image represent brilliant ideas, clarifying thoughts, insights, and sensible reasoning.

DECISION-MAKING

· *Today, the day ahead*—Today is not the day for doubts, indecisiveness, or procrastination. It's best to make a definitive and resolute decision now, at all costs.

· *Today, in love*—When it comes to love, making important decisions together with your partner can be a source of tension. Even if you feel you're in the right, try not to come across as controlling, but rather be open to discussion. What happened to the romance between you two?

· *Today, at work*—Today at work, you might find yourself facing a decision that carries significant responsibility, not only for yourself but also for your colleagues or employees. It's important to rely on your logical reasoning and approach the situation with a professional and objective mindset.

· *Self-reflection*—Dwelling on the past and revisiting unresolved issues can be a two-edged sword. It's wiser to reflect on the present situation before making decisions for the future.

· *A symbol*—Today, you can reflect on the symbol of the barren landscape. This image serves as a reminder that being cold and aloof, especially when combined with harsh words, can push away friends and create a void around you.

Doubt · Calmness

The Two of Swords symbolizes an inability to tap into your intuition,
resulting in difficulty in finding solutions. It stands in stark contrast
to the High Priestess card, which also has the number 2.

Choose what kind of energy you want to draw from the Two of Swords today:
Contradictory Thoughts, Rest, Loneliness

CONTRADICTORY THOUGHTS

· *Today, the day ahead*—If you're faced with a situation today where you're unsure which path to take or which option to choose, try not to overthink or weigh the pros and cons too heavily. Instead, try listening to your innermost feelings—they can often guide you in the right direction.

· *Today, in love*—Whether you're single or in a relationship, you may not feel as loved today as you'd like to be. Are you unsure about your own feelings or doubting your partner's love for you? Before bringing up the issue and risking damaging a healthy relationship, consider waiting it out as it may just be a temporary crisis.

· *Today, at work*—If conflicts arise at work today, it may be worth asking yourself whether you could be partly responsible. Maybe you haven't communicated your needs clearly enough, or perhaps you're feeling a little uncertain yourself. It's probably best to avoid making any major or final decisions for the time being.

· *Self-reflection*—Many Eastern philosophies teach that our thoughts can cloud our connection to our innermost selves. To counteract this, it can be helpful to quiet the mind through meditation. If possible, try to find a small space to meditate today, preferably in silence and darkness.

· *A symbol*—Today, you can reflect on the symbol of the moon in the background. This card depicts a woman who is blindfolded and facing away from the sea and the moon, representing a reluctance or inability to pay attention to intuition, dreams, and coincidences.

REST

· *Today, the day ahead*—Being overly defensive can give others the impression that you're cold or opinionated. It's important to remember that not every situation can be approached with pure rationality. Try to harbor empathy and show a more compassionate side of yourself.

· *Today, in love*—Is there truly a storm brewing in your relationship, or is it possible that a veil of negativity is preventing you from seeing the peaceful moments? Pursuing perfection can often lead to conflict and harm. Rather than arguing, it may be time to settle differences and seek a path forward together.

· *Today, at work*—The work environment can be a difficult place to be if it feels confrontational and tense. It's important to be aware of whom you can trust in such situations. If you can, try to take a day off to focus on yourself and your mental health.

· *Self-reflection*—If life feels like a constant struggle, take a break from the fight and relax. Start by finding peace within yourself first.

· *A symbol*—Take a moment to reflect on the symbolism of crossed swords. They often symbolize the inner turmoil, conflicting ideas, and self-doubt that we experience. In these moments, it's important to take a step back, take a break from the fight, and wait for the storm to pass.

LONELINESS

· *Today, the day ahead*—Today might be a challenging day for you. Are there any issues that are weighing on your mind? Who or what is causing you distress? Is there a problem that's been bothering you, but you can't seem to find a logical solution? Don't isolate yourself; consider reaching out to a trusted friend to talk about your concerns. This can offer a fresh perspective and help you see things more clearly.

· *Today, in love*—Today may not be the best day to fully embrace love. If you have a partner, it might be helpful to explain why you seem distant or emotionally reserved. Sometimes, taking time for yourself to reflect and work through personal issues can be necessary.

· *Today, at work*—On a stressful workday like today, the wisest approach to navigate rivalries among colleagues is to stay neutral. Simply focus on completing your tasks without taking sides or passing judgment. It's best to wait for the storm to pass and avoid getting caught up in unnecessary conflicts.

· *Self-reflection*—Finding inner balance can be challenging when your thoughts and emotions are running wild. To overcome this, it's helpful to break free from your usual patterns and try to see things from a different perspective. This can help shift your mindset and create a more positive outlook, ultimately leading to a greater sense of balance within yourself.

· *A symbol*—Today, reflect on the symbol of the blindfold. It often represents an inability to see reality for what it truly is. Imagine the woman laying down her weapons and removing the blindfold so that she might finally appreciate the beauty of the moonlit night and the immense sea behind her.

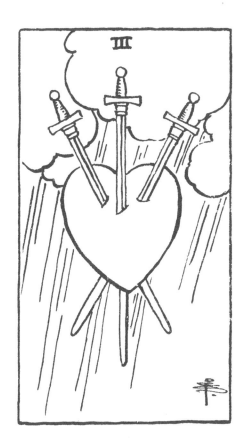

Disenchantment · Hurt Feelings

The Three of Swords is about the importance of painful but necessary awareness. It acknowledges the hurt feelings and thoughts that can disrupt your inner harmony. While this may seem negative, it ultimately serves as a valuable lesson to help you avoid future suffering.

Choose what kind of energy you want to draw from the Three of Swords today:

Disappointment, Disenchantment, Awareness

DISAPPOINTMENT

· *Today, the day ahead*—Things might not go according to plan for you today. Rather than complaining, take a moment to reflect on what went wrong. Did someone or something get in your way? Could you have done more? Alternatively, is it possible that it happened for a reason, and it's for the best?

· *Today, in love*—If you sense that there are dark clouds looming over your relationship, take a moment to reflect on what may have caused them. Did you let your partner down in some way? It's important to identify the root of the issue and consider how you can make things right. There may be something you can do to show your partner that you care and are committed to working through any challenges together.

· *Today, at work*—You may be faced with an unavoidable decision that won't be popular with everyone. If possible, take the time to clarify the reasoning behind your choice and communicate any difficulties you're facing before taking action. Remember, a problem shared is a problem halved, and by working together, you may be able to find a solution that satisfies everyone involved.

· *Self-reflection*—Becoming aware of bitter realities, without illusion or disillusionment, can be painful, but it serves an important purpose. Painful experiences can help you learn from your mistakes and avoid repeating them in the future. It's also important to be mindful of the pressure that this awareness can put on you.

· *A symbol*—Today's symbol for reflection is the dark clouds. It's a reminder that sometimes in life, we have to face difficult times. Behind the clouds the sun is still shining. Remember to be patient and wait for the clouds to clear.

DISENCHANTMENT

· *Today, the day ahead*—If you're hurt by something—or more likely, someone—today, don't pretend it doesn't bother you. There's no use in bottling up your emotions. Acknowledge your pain, express your grievances, let it all out: it won't last forever.

· *Today, in love*—It can be hard to cope with a broken heart, but don't rush the healing process. Take the time to understand why the relationship didn't work out, so you can learn from it and avoid making the same mistakes in the future.

· *Today, at work*—You have clearly put in a lot of effort at work, but unfortunately it seems that it hasn't been enough. Criticism has been rife, and you feel unsupported. This could be a valuable learning experience for you: will you use your energy more efficiently in the future, or will you give up entirely?

· *Self-reflection*—Life is filled with challenges, obstacles, grief, and difficult moments that we all have to navigate. However, if you approach these challenges with reason prevailing over emotion, you can overcome any trial and move forward with your head held high. It's important to remember that you will inevitably have hardships to endure, but by staying grounded in reason, you can face them with courage and determination.

· *A symbol*—Reflecting on the pierced heart symbol today can be a powerful reminder of the spiritual lessons that come with pain. This ancient image is often associated with the idea that swords represent the painful but necessary realizations that shape our spirit and help us grow.

AWARENESS

· *Today, the day ahead*—Communication could be problematic today. If possible, it's best to distance yourself from confrontational people or situations. Remember, sometimes disappointments can provide valuable insights and allow us to see things more clearly.

· *Today, in love*—A wounded heart can be difficult to win back. To heal it, patience, gentleness, and listening are essential. Instead of overthinking, focus on showing more love.

· *Today, at work*—If you want to succeed in a challenging test at work or school today, it's important to be rational and not let your emotions take over. Focus on yourself and don't waste time and energy on people who don't deserve your respect.

· *Self-reflection*—This Arcanum is designed to help you prepare for difficult times with awareness and clarity. No matter what happens, try to stay in control of yourself; don't let yourself be consumed by despair.

· *A symbol*—Today, reflect on the symbol of the rain. If you look behind the big red heart, you can see rain falling heavily. This rain represents the heartbreaking, yet liberating tears shed by those who have torn the veil of illusion from their eyes and are now facing the stark reality of a situation.

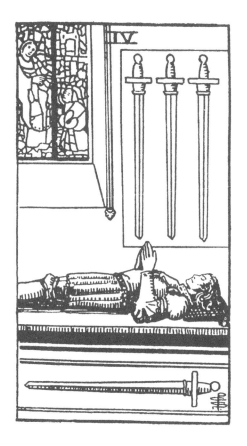

Forced Pause · Immobility

The Four of Swords symbolizes a moment of pause, one that
was unexpected but necessary to reflect on the future and reorganize it.
Emotions are set aside for a time to allow for deep contemplation.

Choose what kind of energy you want to draw from the Four of Swords today:
Recollection, Deadlock, Recovery

RECOLLECTION

· *Today, the day ahead*—This Arcanum invites you to pause and reflect. If possible, clear your schedule today, disconnect from your phone, and take some time for yourself. This strategy can help you identify what truly matters and is essential to you.

· *Today, in love*—This isn't the time to make plans for the future. If your partner appears distant or uninterested, it may be worth exploring their thoughts. Do they need time to reflect, or is there truly nothing left to rekindle the relationship?

· *Today, at work*—Today might be one of those days where it feels like nothing is going right. Your computer might freeze, projects might come to a standstill, and appointments might get postponed. When it seems like the universe is against you, it's best to just go with the flow. Why not use this time to tidy up your workspace and review your schedule?

· *Self-reflection*—It's a good idea to take a break today to give your body and mind a chance to rest and recharge.

· *A symbol*—Today, take a moment to reflect on the symbol of the hands pressed together. This knight with his hands together on his chest represents prayer and detachment from worldly troubles. Emulating this posture can be a great way to restore your inner peace.

DEADLOCK

· *Today, the day ahead*—Today is the perfect day to recharge your batteries and regain your strength. If possible, take a day off to rest and rejuvenate, so that tomorrow you can tackle your tasks and commitments with renewed motivation and determination.

· *Today, in love*—Today, your heart may be weighed down by circumstances that are out of your control. If you are in a relationship, you may have to spend time away from your partner despite your wishes. If you are single, something may prevent you from making new connections. However, remember that tomorrow is a new day and things will be brighter.

· *Today, at work*—Today's workday may be slow and unproductive. Use this downtime to recharge your batteries and develop new plans and strategies.

· *Self-reflection*—If you've been through a stressful period or are recovering from an illness, taking a break from social life (and social media) can be a great way to recharge. Have you ever considered spending time in a serene, spiritual setting?

· *A symbol*—Today, you can reflect on the symbol of the stained glass window. Take a closer look at the window depicted in this Arcanum; it resembles the stained glass windows found in churches and represents the enlightenment that comes from introspection and prayer.

RECOVERY

· *Today, the day ahead*—If you have been feeling sluggish since you woke up this morning, it might be helpful to take a mineral supplement. Have a fruit and vegetable smoothie or a green juice. It would be best to avoid activities that are too strenuous.

· *Today, in love*—Sometimes, trying to repair a damaged relationship can feel like an unnecessary burden. However, if you still sense love between you and your partner, it's worthwhile to take some time to reflect on what went wrong and work toward a solution.

· *Today, at work*—Use this workday, which may be a bit slow, to forward plan and tie up any loose ends.

· *Self-reflection*—Getting a good night's sleep is a real blessing for restoring both mental and physical energy, especially if you have been through an illness or are recovering from one. If you can, try to recall your dreams and see what message they may be conveying.

· *A symbol*—Take a moment today to reflect on the symbolism of the knight lying still. In the past, becoming a knight required a lifetime of dedication to hard work and perilous tasks. This knight lying still serves as a reminder that it's essential to take breaks from life's difficulties to manage them more effectively.

Defeat · Humiliation

The Five of Swords shows a scene of defeat, with the losers appearing
to slink away in shame and the supposed winner looking on with a sneer.
But is this really a victory? Perhaps the real winners are those who
choose to walk away from an unnecessary battle.

Choose what kind of energy you want to draw from the Five of Swords today:

Failure, Pride, War and Peace

FAILURE

· *Today, the day ahead*—Try to steer clear of any kind of disagreement. If you must confront someone, don't go in assuming you have the upper hand; you may end up feeling embarrassed and hurt.

· *Today, in love*—When a relationship ends, one person is usually more hurt than the other. Taking revenge is not the best way to handle the situation, so it's best to just move on and try to heal. That's the wisest and least draining approach.

· *Today, at work*—Be mindful of your surroundings at work today. Not everyone has your best interests in mind, and someone could try to take advantage of you. Don't let them push you around; if they try to provoke you, don't take the bait and don't back down. Fight for yourself.

· *Self-reflection*—Even the strongest people will experience bitter defeats. There are broken pieces on the path of each of us, We can leave them behind or pick them up and put them back together again. What emerges will be a warning for the future.

· *A symbol*—The symbol you can reflect on today is the loser. The man walking away with bowed head represents the humiliation one feels after a defeat. It is a feeling we all experience at one time or another in life, teaching us to understand that one cannot always win and that there is no point in bragging about one's successes or mocking those who have not succeeded.

PRIDE

· *Today, the day ahead*—It's best not to take anything for granted today or declare victory too soon: you might pay dearly for your arrogance. Don't get too far ahead of yourself; stay humble.

· *Today, in love*—It's not worth staying in a state of resentment; it's better to make amends and try to heal any hurt feelings. In relationships, what matters most is having a strong and lasting bond, not just fleeting emotions.

· *Today, at work*—Why the know-it-all attitude? It's important to keep in mind that constantly trying to show off to colleagues, classmates, or professional partners may not garner admiration, but rather have the opposite effect. Be mindful and watch your back.

· *Self-reflection*—This card serves as a reminder to let go of any grudges you may be holding on to, to lay down your arms, and to practice forgiveness toward yourself and others. You should also remember to not be too quick to judge, as you may be judged in the same way.

· *A symbol*—The symbol for today is the swaggerer. This is the person who smirks as they watch others walk away, representing arrogance. It's important to remember that since winning isn't always possible, those who boast about their fleeting successes are bound to be disappointed in the end.

WAR AND PEACE

· *Today, the day ahead*—If possible, try to repair relationships with people you once loved but have since grown apart from. Don't worry if your attempts are met with rejection; at least you can say that you made an effort.

· *Today, in love*—All relationships have their ups and downs, but what's crucial is that both partners have an opportunity to explain themselves and express their point of view. If only one person is always the dominant voice, it could indicate that the relationship lacks balance and harmony.

· *Today, at work*—The atmosphere at work may not be the most serene. Relationships can be strained, and competition can be excessive. Some people may try to outdo each other. If possible, it's best to avoid getting caught up in these dynamics. However, if you do find yourself in the thick of it, be prepared to use all the tools at your disposal and defend yourself with a healthy dose of cynicism. As the saying goes, "What goes around, comes around".

· *Self-reflection*—This card encourages you to not wallow in self-pity when you experience defeat and to not be concerned with what others think. If something is causing you distress, just remove yourself from the situation.

· *A symbol*—Today's symbol for reflection is the cloudy sky. Although the battle may appear to be over, the clouds hovering over the field suggest that conflict may resume. Therefore, it's advisable to remain vigilant and not let your guard down.

Unchartered Land · Aiding Change

The Six of Swords symbolizes the journey from one circumstance to another. The path ahead may not always be clear or certain, but with support from those around you, you can face your fears with greater ease and confidence.

Choose what kind of energy you want to draw from the Six of Swords today:

Fear of Change, Overcoming Obstacles, Journey

FEAR OF CHANGE

· *Today, the day ahead*—You may need to make some big changes in your life today. Try to stay positive and embrace them, especially if they affect not only you but your entire family.

· *Today, in love*—Relationships, just like people, can change, evolve, mature, and often involve tough decisions. If you're going through a breakup, it's important to reach out to someone you trust, such as a friend, family member, or therapist, who can provide you with the support you need.

· *Today, at work*—If you're feeling overwhelmed by a new task at work and don't know how to proceed, don't be afraid to reach out for help. Ask someone who you think may have more experience than you for guidance. It's always wise to get a second opinion.

· *Self-reflection*—This card serves as a reminder to live each stage of your life with strength and courage, even though you don't know what the future holds. Nothing is permanent, so make the most of every moment.

· *A symbol*—Today, you can reflect on the symbol of the far shore. In the distance, you can make out a shoreline, but you don't know what awaits you there. It could be welcoming, or it could be hostile, but it is there, and it is calling out to those who are willing to take the risk and venture into the unknown. It symbolizes the future and the courage it takes to face it, whatever may come.

OVERCOMING OBSTACLES

· *Today, the day ahead*—If you face the day unhurriedly, handling one problem at a time, methodically and rationally, perhaps by being guided, you will arrive in the evening exhausted but satisfied with what you were able to accomplish.

· *Today, in love*—If a couple can keep their common goals in sight, any difficulties in their relationship can be overcome. It is especially important to do this if you have children or other people who rely on you, so you can look to the future and leave any past issues behind.

· *Today, at work*—If you are determined to succeed at work, don't let obstacles or the time it takes to overcome them discourage you. Keep pushing forward, even if you have to go against the current. With that kind of commitment, you will be able to achieve your goals.

· *Self-reflection*—Remember, there's nothing that can't be faced, no obstacle that can't be overcome, and no uncertainty that isn't worth experiencing, especially when you have people who believe in you by your side.

· *A symbol*—Reflecting on the symbol of the long paddle today can be a reminder of your ability to use intelligence, caution, and self-sacrifice to tackle difficult challenges. Not only does the paddle help you move forward, it also allows you to feel the bottom of the waterway.

JOURNEY

· *Today, the day ahead*—Today is the perfect day to start a new adventure. It doesn't matter where you go, how long it takes, or what you find when you get there. What's important is that you enjoy the journey, and it's always better when you have someone to share it with.

· *Today, in love*—A trip, tour, or cruise can be a great way to rekindle the romance in your relationship. Whether you're in a couple or single, you'll have the opportunity to create special memories with your partner or even meet someone new.

· *Today, at work*—You may hear news today that you have to relocate or go on a business trip. No matter where you have to go, take the chance to experience something new and have a change of scenery—but don't set your expectations too high.

· *Self-reflection*—Have you ever considered embarking on a journey of self-discovery? You may uncover vast plains, dark caves, soaring mountains, or unfathomable depths. There are parts of yourself that you never knew existed. But always remember, it's the journey that matters, not the destination.

· *A symbol*—Today, reflect on the symbol of the boat. This ancient symbol of initiation represents the journey of souls through the cycle of life.

Dishonesty · Slyness

The Seven of Swords symbolizes deceit and a tendency
to avoid taking responsibility. It suggests a person's capacity
to deceive and manipulate others.

Choose what kind of energy you want to draw from the Seven of Swords today:

Slyness, Evading Issues, Prudence

SLYNESS

· *Today, the day ahead*—Pay close attention to the people you'll be dealing with today. Don't let yourself be taken advantage of—stay alert and vigilant!

· *Today, in love*—Are you certain that your partner is committed to following through on their promises? Did they just make these promises to get what they wanted and placate you for the time being? Clarify this right away.

· *Today, at work*—The work environment isn't particularly peaceful, and the relationship between colleagues and associates is shady. If you don't want others to take credit for your projects, it's best to keep them to yourself.

· *Self-reflection*—Today, it's important to ask yourself if you're being genuine with others and yourself. How sincere are your intentions? Can you be trusted? Keep in mind that you reap what you sow.

· *A symbol*—Today's symbol for reflection is the thief. This sneaky character, with a sly grin, appears to be stealing other people's swords. It represents human shrewdness and acts as a reminder that even the most decent of us may occasionally resort to cheating for personal gain.

EVADING ISSUES

· *Today, the day ahead*—Stop wasting your time on pointless activities and face reality. Take a deep breath and get rid of the weight you're carrying. Roll up your sleeves and tackle the situation head-on.

· *Today, in love*—If you're looking for a genuine, honest relationship, it's time to be open and honest about your intentions. Don't keep any secrets or doubts hidden away—it won't do either of you any good.

· *Today, at work*—It's time to face the music and take responsibility for the difficult issue you've been avoiding. Don't try to shift the blame onto others—you know that's not right. Ignorance is no excuse in the eyes of the law.

· *Self-reflection*—Our minds naturally try to avoid what makes us uncomfortable, but this doesn't solve our problems; it only makes them worse. It may be painful, but it's better to confront difficult issues directly, rather than letting them fester.

· *A symbol*—Today's symbol to reflect on is the encampment. In the background, we can see a field of tents and people camping, representing the social responsibilities and burdens that we often try to avoid.

PRUDENCE

· *Today, the day ahead*—Today, be mindful of your actions and the people you choose to be around, as a false step could have serious repercussions.

· *Today, in love*—If you're getting to know someone new or starting a relationship, it's important to be mindful and aware that not all that glitters is gold.

· *Today, at work*—Be on the lookout for a particularly savvy colleague or customer at work today. If you're signing any contracts, make sure to read through all the details thoroughly. Be wary of any potential fraud or deceit!

· *Self-reflection*—If you have a dream that you cherish, keep it close to your heart and guard it carefully. Sometimes revealing our deepest aspirations to others can hinder their realization.

· *A symbol*—The symbol to reflect on today is tiptoeing. The character's attitude appears stealthy and silent, representing the need to move shrewdly and cautiously during delicate situations.

Confinement · Limiting Beliefs

The Eight of Swords refers to the concept of limitations, whether imposed voluntarily or involuntarily. It may represent a transitional phase during which you are unable to act until a particular situation is resolved or an obstacle is removed. Alternatively, it may signify a status quo that seems impossible to overcome, leaving you feeling stuck and unable to find a way forward.

Choose what kind of energy you want to draw from the Eight of Swords today:
Prohibition, Control, Sacrifice

PROHIBITION

· *Today, the day ahead*—You may find yourself unwilling to leave your home due to some unforeseen circumstances. Is it a problem that is beyond your control, or are you simply not feeling up to going out? If this situation persists for an extended period of time, it would be advisable to consider finding a solution.

· *Today, in love*—Today's situation is preventing you from having a peaceful relationship. Whether it's psychological blocks or outside interference, you need to address the issue quickly if you don't want it escalating into an unsolvable issue.

· *Today, at work*—If you feel that your workplace is constraining you and not allowing you to fully express your ideas or potential, it may be time to consider making a change.

· *Self-reflection*—If you're feeling stuck and overwhelmed with the lack of prospects for the future, take some time to investigate the root cause of this crisis. Ask yourself if it could be due to any unfounded fears or inhibitions that you may be holding on to. It may be that by letting go of these, you can make progress and move forward.

· *A symbol*—Today, you can contemplate the symbolism of the cage. The swords are arranged like the bars of a cage, with a woman in the center who doesn't seem to realize that there is a way out. This card is a reminder that some of the limitations we experience may be self-imposed illusions, rather than actual barriers.

CONTROL

· *Today, the day ahead*—Today, you may feel confined by your environment, with a heavy sense of restrictions, regulations, and prohibitions that leave you feeling stifled. If you're not someone who's willing to make compromises or give up certain things, it may be time to break free from the oppressive restraints and suffocating connections that are keeping you back.

· *Today, in love*—If your relationship feels like a prison, it's time to take a step back and ask yourself a few questions. Are you feeling controlled by an overly jealous partner? If so, it's clear that this isn't a healthy relationship. Or do you need more freedom? If so, it's likely that you've grown tired of the relationship. Either way, staying in this situation in no longer sustainable.

· *Today, at work*—When it comes to important decisions at work, it is advisable to avoid making them today. A temporary lack of perspective may cause you to view things from an incorrect standpoint. It's best to wait until you have a clearer understanding before making any significant choices.

· *Self-reflection*—If you truly aspire to become the master of your life, it's essential to ask yourself what prejudices or preconceptions may be hindering your personal growth. Don't become enslaved by your own thoughts; strive to keep an open mind and broaden your perspective!

· *A symbol*—Today's symbol to reflect upon is bondage. The bindings wrapped around the woman symbolize the restrictions and boundaries that you may be facing, whether you have chosen them or not. It's up to you, and no one else, to break free from these restrictions.

SACRIFICE

· *Today, the day ahead*—Sometimes it's necessary to make tough decisions to achieve something great. Put in the hard work today and you'll be able to reap the rewards tomorrow.

· *Today, in love*—If your partner is going through a difficult time due to circumstances beyond their control, it's important to prioritize their needs and provide them with the support they need to get through it.

· *Today, at work*—You may not have the freedom to do what you want due to work or study commitments. Remember that this is only a temporary phase and once you have completed the tasks that are taking up so much of your time, you will be able to focus on more enjoyable activities. Make sure that this doesn't become a long-term issue.

· *Self-reflection*—At times, you may feel like you're holding yourself back from true happiness due to a sense of obligation, a strict upbringing, or psychological barriers. However, it's important not to let these assumptions limit you, as you have the freedom to be your own person.

· *A symbol*—Today, take a moment to reflect on the symbolism of a swamp. In the far distance, you can see a fortress with a castle perched on top, but the foreground is characterized by soggy land and a gloomy sky. This image represents a time of limitation and difficulty, as you eagerly anticipate brighter days ahead.

Anguish · Regret

The Nine of Swords symbolizes the presence of fears, anxieties, and
troubling thoughts, suggesting the need to address these issues promptly.

Choose what kind of energy you want to draw from the Nine of Swords today:

Worries, Guilt, Fears for the Future

WORRIES

· *Today, the day ahead*—If you woke up feeling exhausted and out of sorts, it's clear that the previous night didn't provide you with the rest you needed. If you're struggling with insomnia or can't switch off your thoughts, you might want to try some meditation or take an herbal sleep aid.

· *Today, in love*—There are two possibilities: either your relationship is going through a rough phase, or it has ended, and you're finding it hard to move on. Remember that it's still too early to start rebuilding your life, and you need time to come to terms with the absence of your partner, like going through any other grieving process.

· *Today, at work*—Are you going through a highly stressful time at work, to the extent that you can't seem to switch off even when you get back home? The thoughts and responsibilities are just too much to handle, and it's not your fault if things aren't going well at the moment. Don't worry, just hang in there till it passes.

· *Self-reflection*—When times are tough, it can feel like the problems are insurmountable and that there's no hope in sight. Don't be afraid to reach out to someone you trust for help; it's okay to not be able to handle everything on your own.

· *A symbol*—The symbol to contemplate today is that of the threatening blades. The swords looming over this person represent unresolved problems, existential anxieties, and guilt, all of which hinder your ability to live and sleep peacefully.

GUILT

· *Today, the day ahead*—If you can't find peace with something you've done, remember that dwelling on it won't change anything—it will only hurt you. Mistakes from the past can be used as a lesson to help you avoid making the same mistakes in the future.

· *Today, in love*—If you feel like something is preventing you from having a peaceful relationship, it's important to have the courage to talk to your partner about it. It can be hard to open up, but it's the only way to get it off your chest and work through the issues.

· *Today, at work*—It's understandable that you feel overwhelmed and like you're not meeting expectations today, but maybe you're expecting too much of yourself?

· *Self-reflection*—Have you taken a path that isn't right for you and now regret it? Don't worry, it's okay to turn back or change direction. Everyone makes mistakes, so don't be too hard on yourself!

· *A symbol*—Reflect on the symbolism of the blanket today. If you take a closer look, you will see that it is adorned with roses and astrological symbols. These symbols represent the opportunities that life has to offer; it is up to you to figure out how to apply them to your life.

FEARS FOR THE FUTURE

· *Today, the day ahead*—You should not be so distressed! Don't let negative thoughts take over—the more you focus on them, the more trouble they'll bring. Take a deep breath and try to stay positive. Those who fret less live more peacefully.

· *Today, in love*—Past mistakes, traumas, and heartbreak may prevent you from opening your heart to love. It's understandable that letting go of old patterns is difficult, but it's not impossible. Once you can leave the past behind, you can look forward to a new, brighter future.

· *Today, at work*—Perhaps it's not the ideal time to plan for the future, make ambitious investments, and set long-term goals. However, could it be possible that things at work are not as bad as you perceive them to be? Could it be that you're being a little too pessimistic?

· *Self-reflection*—If you find yourself feeling exhausted and overwhelmed, alternating between periods of sadness and anxiety, it may be time to speak to a therapist who can help you find peace and gain a healthier perspective.

· *A symbol*—Today's symbol for reflection is the hands over eyes. Notice the woman's body language: she isn't blindfolded, and the threatening blades aren't actually harming her. Instead, she is covering her own eyes with her hands and unable to let go. Her posture represents the tendency to become trapped in our own thoughts and worries.

Voluntary Termination · Radical Change

The Ten of Swords symbolizes a strong urge to finish something or sever ties with someone. It is only through this that you can be reborn and create a new path for the future.

Choose what kind of energy you want to draw from the Ten of Swords today:

Clean Cut, Past Wounds, Exhaustion and Recovery

CLEAN CUT

· *Today, the day ahead*—Today is the perfect time to make a bold and drastic change. Your decisions may appear extreme and even harsh to some, but deep down you know they are absolutely necessary.

· *Today, in love*—If you're going through the end of a relationship, whether it was your choice or not, it's likely not the happiest time in your life. But it had to happen this way; by facing the grief, you can open yourself up to finding love again.

· *Today, at work*—Today, a project that you have put a lot of effort into may not be successful. Before giving up completely, consider the possibility of altering your approach.

· *Self-reflection*—It looks like you're not willing to settle for anything less than your best right now. Don't worry about what other people think—focus on what works for you and don't be afraid to go all in.

· *A symbol*—The symbol to reflect on today is the black sky. This dark and gloomy sky represents the need to confront your deepest fears and come to terms with the end of a cycle. Only after you go through the darkness can you truly experience the light.

PAST WOUNDS

· *Today, the day ahead*—You knew you had to make a change, and you did. You have a clean slate— there's no going back now. Take a moment to process what you've done, but don't linger too long—it's time to look forward.

· *Today, in love*—The end of a love affair can be incredibly painful. It may seem like you'll never get through it, but you will. To make it through with your dignity intact, it's best to avoid jumping into a new relationship or seeking revenge against your former partner.

· *Today, at work*—Some of the decisions you made may have been met with criticism. Explain why you chose to act the way you did, provide evidence to support your strategy, and be prepared for any potential backlash.

· *Self-reflection*—It's common for those who make drastic changes to their lives overnight to feel misunderstood. If you've recently made a radical choice, it's possible that some people you considered friends may distance themselves from you. It's important to remember that the problem lies not with you or the decisions you've made, but rather with some people's incapacity to respect others' choices.

· *A symbol*—Today's symbol to reflect upon is the swords in the back. This unfortunate character is stabbed by swords, lying seemingly lifeless face down on the ground, yet not a drop of blood is shed. The swords in this case symbolize the hurtful words, malicious gossip, and unfair judgments (in other words, the backstabbing) of those who think they are always right.

EXHAUSTION AND RECOVERY

· *Today, the day ahead*—If you've been through a difficult period, it's time to pick yourself back up. It may not be easy, especially if you've been through a lot, but a new chapter of your life is beginning and it's worth approaching it with a positive attitude. Believe in yourself—you can do this!

· *Today, in love*—Stop dwelling on the past and being so hard on yourself for the mistakes you've made. Don't you realize that by doing this, you're pushing away people who could be interested in you? Let go of that victim attitude—it's not attractive in the least!

· *Today, at work*—Are you contemplating significant changes to your business or are you resolute in your determination to transform your career and lifestyle? Regardless of the path you choose, it's important to acknowledge that the future will be different from the past, but there's potential for it to be even better.

· *Self-reflection*—Recovering from exhaustion cannot be achieved in just a few minutes; it requires time and, above all, a genuine desire to heal. The more arduous the challenges were, the more strenuous the recovery process will be. Thus, it's crucial to give yourself permission to take a break and prioritize rest.

· *A symbol*—Today's symbol for reflection is lying face down. The image shows a man lying on the ground, face down, stabbed by multiple swords, yet there is no visible blood. It is uncertain whether he is unable or unwilling to get up. This posture serves as a powerful symbol of the importance of seeking help during times of extreme discouragement.

Vitality · Critical Attitude

The Page of Swords suggests that clarification is needed.
It may not be welcomed, but it could be beneficial, as it could
provide a chance for personal development.

Choose what kind of energy you want to draw from the Page of Swords today:

Curiosity, Conflict, Assertation

CURIOSITY

· *Today, the day ahead*—Today, you have an abundance of mental and physical energy, fueling your desire for action and hunger for knowledge. It's an ideal day to attend exhibitions, conventions, book presentations, and gallery openings.

· *Today, in love*—If you're single today, why not take the chance to meet someone new and exciting? Don't let this opportunity pass you by—get to know them better and see where it leads.

· *Today, at work*—You are a naturally curious person, and you thrive on intellectual work and study. You don't shy away from mental challenges, but try to avoid overwhelming your colleagues or professors with too many questions!

· *Self-reflection*—Significant and swift transformations in your life are on the horizon. Thanks to your intelligence and willingness to try new things, you'll be able to embrace them with ease. Let yourself take the plunge.

· *A symbol*—Today, reflect on the symbolism of the birds flying through the sky. They represent the totality of your dreams, hopes, and ambitions. As your mind soars higher, you will become more passionate about life.

CONFLICT

· *Today, the day ahead*—If you receive criticism today, try not to take it personally. Instead, consider it as an opportunity to learn and grow. Keep in mind that constructive criticism, although it may sting, can be valuable in helping you improve. So stay open-minded and receptive to feedback.

· *Today, in love*—There seems to be distance between you and your partner. Is it just today? Or has it been like this for a while? If it is the latter, and you and your partner are constantly criticizing and reprimanding each other, it's time to figure out if the problem can be overcome or if it's time to move on.

· *Today, at work*—Do you feel like you're constantly being criticized at work and that there's a lot of hostility around you? Have you tried talking to the people around you to see if there's anything you can do to better meet their needs? Or is it that they can't keep up with you?

· *Self-reflection*—We often have an innate desire to attempt great feats, travel far distances, and pursue goals that may only exist in our minds. But we fail to recognize that what we truly need is often right in front of us.

· *A symbol*—Today, take a moment to reflect on the symbol of the wind. Who is the Page fighting? Is he fighting an invisible adversary, or is he simply battling the wind, which is causing his hair to ruffle? This image serves as a reminder to not worry about issues that are insignificant or even imaginary.

ASSERTATION

· *Today, the day ahead*—Today, your mental acuteness will give you the strength to tackle any challenge. You have already achieved so much, don't let anything stand in your way.

· *Today, in love*—Having a sharp wit and a good sense of humor can help you win over anyone. A brilliant mind can be more attractive than a toned body or perfect features.

· *Today, at work*—Advancing in your career requires starting from the bottom and working your way up to senior positions. You possess all the necessary qualities to excel, but it's important not to rush the process. Demonstrating your commitment and skills to those in higher positions can help you stand out and pave the way for future growth opportunities.

· *Self-reflection*—You don't have to be forceful or show unyielding strength to assert your will. It's enough to have a clear understanding of what you want, openly communicate it, and consistently act on it. When you do this, others will naturally adjust and adapt to your desires.

· *A symbol*—The symbol of long hair has come to represent strength and freedom. It harkens back to the story of Samson, whose strength was believed to be contained in his hair, and to the hippie movement's ideals of peace and freedom, which they expressed by allowing their hair to grow long. This is symbolic of the power of thought and the spiritual power that comes from understanding.

Attack · Storm

The Knight of Swords brings a chill to the air,
signaling a turbulent time ahead. Brace yourself as you prepare
to defend your position with fierce determination.

Choose what kind of energy you want to draw from the Knight of Swords today:

Cold-Heartedness, Determination, Conflict

COLD-HEARTEDNESS

· *Today, the day ahead*—The wind is howling, is a storm brewing? Are you ready to bring down a deluge of thunder and lightning? If that's your plan, let it out—but take care not to harm anyone you care about, otherwise you'll come to regret it.

· *Today, in love*—It doesn't make sense or even benefit either party to carry on a relationship that has become cold and distant. There is no way to revive the spark; it would be wise to seek out other options for finding companionship.

· *Today, at work*—You should maintain a cool, collected, and even slightly detached attitude if you want to successfully face any challenges that might come up at work today. Be prepared to be scrutinized and to receive criticism.

· *Self-reflection*—Before you make impulsive decisions or ones driven solely by your desire to rush and expend your energy unnecessarily, it would be wise to take a moment to contemplate and concentrate on your true objectives.

· *A symbol*—The ancients were well familiar with the power of the north wind: it can strip trees of their foliage, freeze crops, and wreak havoc on homes with its icy chill. When the north wind blows, all we can do is take cover and wait for it to pass. Just like the north wind, intemperance can take away our rational judgment and devastate the relationships around us. Reflecting on this symbol today can serve as a reminder of the dangers of recklessness.

DETERMINATION

· *Today, the day ahead*—Today your assertive attitude will help you find solutions quickly. It's undeniable that you are smart, but be careful with your words if you don't want to hurt anyone's feelings.

· *Today, in love*—Your thoughts may be running at a million miles a minute, but your partner might not be able to keep up with you. If you want to keep progressing together, try to tone down your self-centeredness a bit.

· *Today, at work*—No matter how many obstacles you have to overcome, how hard you have to work, or what tactics you need to use to succeed in your job, you are unwavering in your ambition and ready to do whatever it takes. Just remember to stay compassionate and kind in your pursuit of success.

· *Self-reflection*—Having tenacity doesn't mean you won't ever stumble, but rather that you'll rebound when you do, stay resilient when times get tough, and keep your sights set on the objective, no matter how distant it may seem.

· *A symbol*—The symbol to contemplate today is the unsheathed sword. It stands for the power to overthrow anything that stands in the way of your success. It can be a two-edged sword: if you are too self-serving, you may end up isolated.

CONFLICT

· *Today, the day ahead*—Today you anticipate coming into conflict with someone. No matter how passionate the other person may be, your quick wit will be a surefire way to win. In any argument, it is essential to never resort to offensive language or, even more serious, physical violence.

· *Today, in love*—This card anticipates a time of conflict in love. It is key to determine whether this is a minor argument or a full-blown battle. How much damage are you prepared to inflict, and how much are you prepared to suffer?

· *Today, at work*—Are there any issues between coworkers in the workplace, small or large, that cause tension and hostility? If you can put a stop to it, do your best to defuse the situation. If not, try to keep your distance and not let it affect you too much.

· *Self-reflection*—Conflicts are not always avoidable, especially conflicts within ourselves. Sometimes we need to face the uncomfortable truth to reach a satisfactory resolution.

· *A symbol*—The symbol of armor is something to think about today. It represents the importance of creating a protective shield, both physically and mentally, from the challenges that life throws our way.

Independence · Sense of Humor

The Queen of Swords represents an individual—typically a woman, but not always—who is intelligent, independent, and well-educated. This person may also come across as somewhat cold or aloof.

Choose what kind of energy you want to draw from the Queen of Swords today:

Independence, Humor, Pomposity

INDEPENDENCE

· *Today, the day ahead*—Today would be a great day to visit a museum or catch one of those arthouse films your family enjoys. Consider inviting your most intellectual friend to join you for some company!

· *Today, in love*—Lately, you may be feeling that romantic gestures and displays of affection are less important to you in a relationship. Instead, you're looking for meaningful conversations and intellectual stimulation. Without these things, you'd rather be alone.

· *Today, at work*—You have very clear ideas at work, and your organizational skills make it easy for you to achieve a leadership position. This is an especially favorable day for those who are self-employed.

· *Self-reflection*—Sure, you're self-reliant, intelligent, and capable of solving your problems on your own. But there's nothing wrong with asking for help or seeking out some company every once in a while. Even for tough individuals like yourself, loneliness can take its toll over time.

· *A symbol*—Today's symbol for reflection is the crown with butterflies. At first glance, this Queen may come across as a little intimidating and give off a cold or austere impression. However, if you take a closer look, her crown is decorated with graceful butterflies. This symbol represents the power of the mind— the lighter and more positive the thoughts, the farther they can reach.

HUMOR

· *Today, the day ahead*—This isn't the time to be sulking. That doesn't mean that there aren't any problems—quite the contrary—but if you tackle them with a positive attitude, they won't seem so daunting.

· *Today, in love*—If you have a partner, try to plan an activity that will pique both of your curiosities and make you laugh today. If you are single, you may be in the mood for an unconventional and lighthearted relationship, at least for the time being.

· *Today, at work*—Adding a touch of healthy humor can alleviate a stressful and mentally taxing atmosphere. If you work in a position where you interact with colleagues, clients, students, or patients, make an effort to show a positive attitude and smile—after all, there's nothing more contagious than good humor!

· *Self-reflection*—A person who can handle difficulties with ease, not take themselves too seriously, and accept the ups and downs of life with a sense of irony is truly intelligent.

· *A symbol*—The symbol for reflection today is the image of the clouds. Take a closer look at the picture and you will notice that clouds are present both in the sky and on the Queen's mantle. They symbolize thoughts that can drift by gracefully and unnoticed, or that can lead to intense and transformative experiences, much like a storm.

POMPOSITY

· *Today, the day ahead*—You may receive some criticism today. Others may perceive you as snobbish or opinionated, but in your heart, you simply want to eliminate clichés, mediocrity, and platitudes from your world.

· *Today, in love*—Is your partner or someone you've been seeing recently highly intelligent but also somewhat aloof and reserved? Consider engaging them with activities that pique their curiosity to help them come out of their shell.

· *Today, at work*—Don't confuse authority with pomposity. While authority can establish you as a respected leader, arrogant pomposity can create distance between you and your colleagues. Remember that respect is earned by showing it to others first.

· *Self-reflection*—Don't let a difficult past make you cold-hearted. In fact, it's often the most traumatic experiences that teach us empathy and help us understand others better.

· *A symbol*—Today, reflect on the symbol of the sword held up high and straight in the right hand, which is also seen in the Justice card. This sword is not meant to be a weapon of destruction, but rather a tool to cut away what no longer serves us or what causes us harm.

KING of SWORDS.

Moral Integrity · Willpower

The King of Swords is often portrayed as an educated and eloquent individual, who is quick to action. He may act as a mediator or someone who comes up with successful ideas due to his ability to speak persuasively.

Choose what kind of energy you want to draw from the King of Swords today:

Acumen, Freedom, Leadership

ACUMEN

· *Today, the day ahead*—This day calls for you to be alert, active, and decisive. Let your natural debating skills take the lead and success will be yours.

· *Today, in love*—If you're looking to win someone over, your natural charm can be a powerful asset, but also make sure to be sincere. Take this opportunity to reflect on whether you're truly ready for a serious relationship or if you prefer something more casual.

· *Today, at work*—At work, you can rely on someone who is highly competent and has authority, such as a superior, colleague, or professor. Don't be intimidated by their demeanor, and don't hesitate to approach them.

· *Self-reflection*—You have an inner drive to constantly seek knowledge, understanding, and insights. You cannot simply settle and ignore this feeling, as it is a powerful force within you. Embrace this instinct and take action toward fulfilling it.

· *A symbol*—Today's symbol to contemplate is the slanted sword. This King's sword is angled slightly differently from that of the Queen of Swords (his consort) and Justice. It symbolizes the sharpness needed to make wise, prompt, and successful decisions, no matter what is being judged, but it also shows a certain degree of mercy.

FREEDOM

· *Today, the day ahead*—Today, you may feel a strong desire for freedom and may find it difficult to tolerate any form of constraint, order, or limitation from others. It's important to communicate your needs and boundaries clearly with those around you.

· *Today, in love*—How about injecting some novelty and excitement into your relationship? Share your ideas openly with your partner today and watch them receive them with curiosity and enthusiasm.

· *Today, at work*—This card encourages you to strive for independence in your work. If you've been contemplating starting your own business, today is the opportune time to take those initial steps. If you're an employee, be prepared to tackle a challenging issue that requires a bit of problem-solving.

· *Self-reflection*—Your adventurous spirit craves unexplored territory. Don't just fantasize about it—take action and explore new paths, both externally and within yourself, discovering pristine and unspoiled places along the way.

· *A symbol*—Today, the symbol of untouched lands serves as a reminder of our past and of the importance of preserving nature. It evokes the awe-inspiring beauty of pristine landscapes and emphasizes the urgent need to protect them from human interference. It also serves as a reminder of the wisdom and re-sourcefulness of our ancestors and the importance of showing reverence for the environment.

LEADERSHIP

· *Today, the day ahead*—People are probably coming to you for help today be-cause you've consistently demonstrated your reliability and competence. Don't disregard their pleas for help—you never know when you might need a hand yourself.

· *Today, in love*—If you care for your partner, don't let them down today. They have put their trust in you and look to you for guidance. You are their source of strength and hope in difficult times. Show them your love by being there for them.

· *Today, at work*—Having an analytical mind and problem-solving skills at work can really pay off; you could be commended, promoted, or even put in charge of a team. It's something to be proud of, as you'll be seen as a leader and role model to many.

· *Self-reflection*—Maturity doesn't come with age, it starts the moment some-one learns to take care of their own issues. Having someone to help is great, but it's not a must.

· *A symbol*—Today, reflect on the symbolism of the monolithic throne. Notice the backrest behind the King: it is made of stone, jutting out of the ground, and towering above the edge of the card. It somewhat evokes a menhir or baetylus, those ancient stone monuments used by our ancestors to honor and pray to the gods for help in solving their problems.

REFLECTIONS

TEN STARTER QUESTIONS

For the reader looking for insights into Tarot cards, we have listed here ten suggestions or short answers to help you understand a little more about them or, at least, to satisfy your curiosity. These ten topics—in effect, FAQs—offer bite-sized knowledge in a solid and easy reference guide.

1. WHAT ARE TAROT CARDS AND WHERE DO THEY COME FROM?

Tarot cards are a type of card deck that emerged in Italy, as far as we know, in the mid-fifteenth century. The deck consists of 78 cards (though there exist historical variants of 64 and 97 cards). Up to the eighteenth century, Tarot cards had no direct connection whatsoever to fortune telling. In the 1800s, French Esotericism schools organically linked the various disciplines of Western esoteric traditions (such as astrology, alchemy, Kabbalah, etc.) to Tarot cards. At the same time, more or less independently, Tarot cards began to be used by fortune tellers to read fortunes, simply because "they were more mysterious than normal cards." While the game of Tarot gradually disappeared from history (another curious aspect that few people know: Tarot cards are one of the predecessors of modern Bridge), the reputation of Tarot cards grew as a fortune telling instrument. By the end of the twentieth century, Tarot cards were shifting from traditional fortune telling (such as the fictional version where the fortune teller is seen telling their client, "You will meet a tall, dark stranger...") toward spirituality and psychology.

2. WHAT IS THE COMPOSITION OF A TAROT DECK?

A Tarot deck is made up of two groups of cards: the Minor Arcana and the Major Arcana. The Minor Arcana comprises 56 cards made up of four suits: Cups, Pentacles, Wands, and Swords. For each suit there are ten numbered cards and four court cards (Page, Knight, Queen, and King). Traditionally, each suit is linked to an element and a theme: Cups, water and emotions; Pentacles, earth and materials; Wands, fire and creativity; Swords, air and intellect. The remaining 22 cards are called the Major Arcana. Each card has its own name and specific number (starting from 0, the Fool, up to number XXI, the World).

3. WHY ARE THERE SO MANY DIFFERENT DECKS?

There are two main Tarot "families," and these differ depending on the type of images shown on the cards.

The first family, in chronological order, is the Marseille Tarot, which originates from the cards used in the game in the eighteenth century. In Marseille-style decks, the Justice card is number XI (11) and Strength is number VIII (8). The numbered Minor Arcana cards (the Ace to the Ten of the four suits) are very similar to playing cards, and these are often characterized by stylized drawings known as "pips." For example, the Three of Pentacles simply shows three pentacles and some decorative work.

The second great family is the Waite-Smith Tarot cards, which emerged in England at the beginning of the 1900s. In Waite-Smith-based decks, Strength appears as VIII (8) and Justice as XI (11). Rather than using pips, the numbered cards are all illustrated with scenes related to the meaning of each card.

It is important to remember that outside these two main families, there are literally thousands of different Tarot decks. And, most, if not all of those decks are valid decks. We would suggest that the reader who prefers a more abstract approach to their interpretation use the Marseille Tarot, while the Waite-Smith deck is more an intuitive and visual approach. In all cases, especially for the purposes of our Card of the Day, the only really important thing is that the deck appeals to the reader. Not aesthetically but to the extent that it has a connection with the reader and leads to reflection. If the reader feels it is right, then it is right. If the reader feels it is artificial or distant, then it is not the right deck, regardless of anybody's advice (including this book's advice).

4. HOW DO TAROT CARDS WORK?

Good question. Usually, this question means, "Can Tarot cards predict the future?" as if this was necessarily linked to a supernatural element or as if this was important. We do not wish to appear conceited, but the most basic barometer can "predict the future"—it will rain tomorrow, or not. And this is definitely more accurate than Tarot cards, at least in terms of weather forecasts. Every reader has their own religious or philosophical beliefs about the universe. It is not the job of the Tarot cards—and even less so, this book—to challenge these beliefs. Whatever the individual believes about Tarot cards is completely personal and must be in harmony—not in conflict with—their other convictions. If a person believes in magic, Tarot cards for this person will be magical, but if they do not feel at ease believing this, they are not forced to believe it. The point being that the purpose of Tarot cards is not to make *accurate* readings. The aim is to make *useful* readings (*useful* and *relevant*, according to Barbara Moore, an extraordinary American Tarot author).

There are two theories that explain the essence of Tarot cards in psychological terms, which might be worthwhile knowing. The first arises from Carl Gustav Jung's theory of synchronicity. This theory maintained that two events (often two events occurring at the same time) can be linked to another event without any causal relationship to it. In practical terms, drawing a specific card (or choosing a particular I Ching hexagram) in that very moment is not by chance, but connected in some invisible way to the circumstances that the card reader is experiencing. This is not a rational connection, nor can it be explained by cause/effect, but it does exist. Thus, reading Tarot cards, we use intuition and not rationality, noticing these signs and extracting a meaning from them.

The second and more psychological theory, strictly speaking, is connected to the so-called protective mechanisms. The images on the Tarot cards become sort of mirrors onto which the card reader projects their own subconscious thoughts. The interpretation thus becomes a tool to help you communicate with your deepest inner self: the subconscious, in fact, or—depending on what you believe in—your own spiritual self.

As authors, we are keen to emphasize that it is not that important to know why or how the Tarot cards work. We fall down—and more importantly get back up—without any knowledge of gravitational forces or the complex mathematical equations that govern them.

5. CAN YOU READ YOUR OWN TAROT CARDS?

It used to be said that you could not read your own Tarot cards, and possibly the reader has heard of this saying. There are two main principles for this. The first one being that it was once thought that only through a supernatural talent or by means of in-depth initiatory and esoteric studies could a person approach Tarot cards. The second principle, sadly more influential and robust, is that if people read their own Tarot cards the income of professional fortune tellers would decrease significantly. In any case, today there is no sound reason not to read your own cards. Indeed, most people using Tarot cards actually do this.

However, a few thoughts to consider. When you read your own cards, you need to be aware of two risks that can distort interpretations: desires and fears.

Desires compel us to distort interpretations in a positive way. When we want something, this outcome is forced spontaneously onto the cards even when this likelihood does not exist. Fears act in the opposite manner; they negatively deform interpretation. In the first case, Tarot cards risk becoming like those friends who always say yes to us; they comfort us, but they do not help us improve or grow. In the second case, the Tarot cards become messages of anxiety, bringing out all our insecurities. Either way, this is hardly of any help. When a person feels that they are unable to disentangle their own desires and their own fears from a reading, there is a little effective hack that we feel we should suggest. Instead of pulling out one card, pull out three. The first one will be read in the most positive light (channeling desires into it). The second is read in the most negative light (channeling fears into it). Finally, the third one, by a simple psychological mechanism, will appear as spontaneously balanced. So the interpretation should be focused on this one.

In any case, the Card of the Day method was specifically created for you to read your own cards (so much so that it makes no sense to use it for any another purpose). For this reason, it is immune to the influence of desires and fears and can be applied without using any tricks.

6. GOING BEYOND THE WRITTEN WORD

The reader will see that this book—like almost all books on Tarot cards—at a certain point will provide a series of keywords and meanings for each Arcanum. This is a mandatory step. What is important to be aware of is that this rigid interpretation from a book, which may *seem* like an instruction manual is—in fact—just a step.

The next necessary step is to transform these slightly scholastic and inescapably generic meanings into something useful and relevant to your life. This second step may be difficult at first, just because there is no manual. With practice, not only will it become easy, it will also be emotional.

Let us use a practical example. A card might have suggested meanings of "justice, balance, equity." This, in broad terms, invites us to reflect on the delicate relationship between law and justice, and between justice and compassion. If the aim of the book's explanation is to open the Tarot reader's mind and make them reflect on all the potential meanings of this card, the aim of interpretation is the opposite: to condense all the potential meanings into one practical thought, linked to the reader's direct experience. In this example, we might suggest that the reader, in relation to a problem about which they feel anxiety, not stop at the first impression but create an informed opinion, suspending their judgment for the time being. What really counts is that the reader feels— even if only at a subconscious level—not to be content with the opinion they have formed up to that moment. The message from the cards translates into a seed of knowledge. It becomes a catalyst for a process of growth, enrichment, and, potentially, a solution to a problem. The simplest way to go beyond the semantic meanings is to trust the image. Look at the image, follow your own thoughts and own intuition, abandon yourself to the association of ideas, metaphors, and sensations . . . all of this is part of the interpretation. Thousands of different Tarot decks can have just as many nuances, and each one works uniquely with the reader.

The image—because of the symbols within it, or by virtue of its artistic quality—makes it possible to start from the meanings expressed in words and go beyond them . . . in fact, to go deeper.

7. HOW TO KEEP A TAROT JOURNAL

If—and this "if" is not by chance—the reader wants to gain a deeper understanding of Tarot and to have the time and energy to dedicate to it, the best thing to do would be to keep a journal. Not everyone wants to do something like this. Five minutes a day is a significant space in our lives, and those minutes are valuable. Some, however, may wish to go beyond the Card of the Day. We invite you to devote five minutes of your day to transcribe our own thoughts about the Card of the Day: the meanings chosen, the interpretations that have emerged, the doubts arising. These thoughts, slowly and spontaneously, will start to accumulate. At a certain point, without realizing that you have overstepped a threshold, you will find that your own understanding and knowledge of Tarot cards has have gone on to another level. Accumulation of understanding is different from studying, because it is not something artificial and does not solely rely on the conscious self. It is, on the contrary, a natural ripening process, where seeds are sown every time a card is drawn and which will germinate not on command, but at the right time. This is the very philosophy fundamental to this entire book: a small step every day goes further than an exhausting and intense short burst race.

8. CREATE SACRED SPACE

An important factor in reading Tarot cards is environment. Here, we are not just referring to the external environment, even if obviously noise, distractions, telephone calls, and other stimuli distract and disperse our energy. This is a consideration that is mainly inherent to the psychological space.

Taking "five minutes for yourself" means really doing it. It means stopping, creating an empty space and silence not only around you but inside you. We like the term "sacred space" because it creates the idea of peace, but also presence and attention, which are absolutely necessary to find meaning in a Tarot card.

It may not be easy for many readers to create this space. It is, however, a profoundly healthy process that—independently from the Tarot cards and the Card of the Day—contributes to the individual's spiritual health. Anxiety and panic are often simply illusions. They are habits that we get caught up in, chains created by the complexities of our lives.

Take your own time to be alone for just a moment, to slowly breathe, with the mind devoid of thoughts. It is in these moments, when the ego withdraws and you are at peace, that your presence and attention are at their maximum. All the treasures of the spirit come through harmony.

In practical terms, to use the Card of the Day method, the reader must try to achieve this little moment of self-presence. For this purpose, some Tarot experts use small rituals such as lighting a candle that is extinguished when they are finished with the cards. These rituals, obviously, are simply instruments to help you find this space alone with yourself.

9. HOW TO SHUFFLE THE DECK

On a practical level, you can shuffle your deck in whatever way you like. Tarot cards are fundamentally playing cards. We suggest, however, going easy, for two reasons, the first one being that Tarot cards are often more fragile than playing cards. Going gently avoids damaging the corners and edges, something that often happens. The second reason is that too much energy is a sign of assertiveness—in other words, a conscious presence of one's own body and mind. Shuffling the cards with languid and rhythmic movements—or even spreading them out on a table—can become an instrument to connect with your own intuition, making you more receptive to listening.

When you read the cards as a response to a question, rather than using the Card of the Day method, the moment when you shuffle the cards is also the moment when you reflect on the question and begin to internalize it.

10. HOW TO DRAW A CARD

This too is very simple. For example, after shuffling the cards, divide the deck in two and turn over the top card. This is not the only possible method. Others can be also used; it is not important as long as it feels right to you. At times, it may happen that for some "casual" reason a card emerges on its own. One of the most common cases, to cite one of many, is when one of the cards falls from the deck when shuffling. In these scenarios, it is usually advised to use the card "that jumped out of the deck on its own." Maybe it is a sign, maybe (see point 4) a synchronicity.

The next piece of advice we would like to share with our readers is: don't abuse the Tarot. The Card of the Day is a good method. And if a question comes up, it is good to read the cards. But too many questions create an excessive dependency on Tarot, which generally does not lead to anything beneficial. We can't get clear, unambiguous winning lottery number results from the Tarot cards (a frequent joke among experts, albeit regretful).

Tarot cards lead us more toward a sort of wisdom that we can internalize, a process that needs time and harmony to deliver results and knowledge. The healthiest path is "not too much, nor too little."